PRINCETON STUDIES IN INTERNATIONAL FINANCE

No. 71, November 1991

ECONOMIC REFORM IN THE SOVIET UNION: PAS DE DEUX BETWEEN DISINTEGRATION AND MACROECONOMIC DESTABILIZATION

DANIEL GROS

AND

ALFRED STEINHERR

INTERNATIONAL FINANCE SECTION

DEPARTMENT OF ECONOMICS
PRINCETON UNIVERSITY
PRINCETON, NEW JERSEY

INTERNATIONAL FINANCE SECTION
EDITORIAL STAFF

Peter B. Kenen, *Director (on leave)*
Giuseppe Bertola, *Acting Director*
Margaret B. Riccardi, *Editor*
Lillian Spais, *Editorial Aide*
Lalitha H. Chandra, *Subscriptions and Orders*

Library of Congress Cataloging-in-Publication Data

Gros, Daniel, 1955-
   Economic reform in the Soviet Union : pas de deux between disintegration and macroeconomic destabilization / by Daniel Gros and Alfred Steinherr.
   p. cm.—(Princeton studies in international finance, ISSN 0081-8070 ; no. 71)
   Includes bibliographical references.
   ISBN 0-88165-243-1 (pbk.) : $9.00
   1. Soviet Union—Economic policy—1986-   2. Soviet Union—Economic conditions—1985- I. Steinherr, Alfred. II. Title. III. Series.
HC336.26G79 1991
338.947'009'048—dc20   90-41160
                                                                              CIP

Printed in the United States of America by Princeton University Press at Princeton, New Jersey

International Standard Serial Number: 0081-8070
International Standard Book Number: 0-88165-243-1
Library of Congress Catalog Card Number: 91-41160

It was the best of times, it was the worst of times, it was the age of wisdom, it was the age of foolishness, it was the epoque of belief, it was the epoque of incredulity, . . . we had everything before us, we had nothing before us, we were all going direct to Heaven, we were all going direct the other way.

Dickens, *A Tale of Two Cities*

PREFACE

I do not ordinarily write prefaces to the publications of the International Finance Section, but a few words are needed in this instance. The final draft of this Study was received on August 14, five days before events in Moscow irrevocably changed the political and economic future of the Soviet Union. Although the situation there continues to change rapidly, I decided to publish this Study without inviting the authors to bring it up to date or altering their prophetic introductory remarks. The analysis provided by this Study is even more helpful today than when it was drafted in helping us to understand the problems and choices facing the republics, the center, and those in the outside world who seek to give assistance. Although the vital decisions will be made on political grounds, there is reassuring evidence in this Study that economic autonomy is viable and sensible for some of the republics.

PETER B. KENEN, *Director*
International Finance Section

CONTENTS

LIST OF TABLES

1 INTRODUCTION

In 1991, Soviet citizens may have seen only the worst of times, rather than the best, as the initial euphoria about perestroika waned to make room for pervasive gloom. This gloom has certainly been justified. Partial reforms, hastily prepared and often contradictory, have flooded the country, embodied in laws that have not been implemented. The country has been deeply divided on fundamental policies and the central government has excelled in brinkmanship to avoid the worst of macroeconomic destabilization. Whatever the eventual outcome, present uncertainties are tremendous: nobody can exclude a conservative backlash under military leadership, a repudiation of a fundamental reform generalizing market principles, or a splitting up of the Union. Control over the country's economy has slipped from the hands of the Communist Party and its central institutions, and the economy is in a state of disintegration. The seriousness of this disintegration is difficult to ascertain with precision in view of the doubtful quality of Soviet statistics. Bearing this proviso in mind, here and elsewhere in this paper, we attempt a brief overview.

Although the loss of central control, the accompanying uncertainties, and the timing of political and economic reforms are largely responsible for the present disintegration, there are deeper and older roots to the problem. Soviet statistics tend to have a positive growth bias. But, using the more realistic estimations of the Commission of the European Communities (1990c, chap. 2), it is clear that the Soviet growth rate has been declining quite steadily. After an average annual growth rate of –0.6 percent (officially, 4.7 percent) of net material product (NMP, the "socialist" measure of output) during the 1940s, an exceptionally high annual growth of 9.3 percent (officially, 10.3 percent) was achieved during the 1950s. The rate declined to 4.2 percent (officially, 7 percent) during the 1960s, 2.1 percent (officially, 4.9 percent) during the 1970s, and 0.6 percent (officially, 3.6 percent) during the 1980s.

This negative trend accelerated, with the full extent of mismanagement becoming fully apparent only after 1989. The country has entered a deep recession and is confronted with growing economic disequilibria.

    For discussions and comments, we thank Paul de Grauwe, Horst Feuerstein, Jacques Girard, Hans-Harald Jahn, Jean Pisani-Ferry, and an anonymous referee.

Inflation, officially always zero, is now admitted and is accelerating (7.5 percent, even when using official prices). A sustained high government budget deficit (equivalent to 14 percent of NMP) has emerged, and the Soviet authorities have estimated the size of the monetary overhang at R 165 billion, which, though over 15 percent of output, is considerably lower than the R 300 billion estimated by Western observers. In order to stem these financial disequilibria, Soviet authorities have reduced investment financed from the central budget. They have also proceeded with largely ineffective and unpopular partial currency reforms aimed at confiscating the cash balances of the underground economy.

The decline of NMP during 1990 is estimated to have been 4 percent, but, according to some government sources, production was down by 50 percent in January 1991 compared to the year before. Investment during 1990 declined by 25 percent. The grain harvest reached a record level, but inadequate handling, transport, and storage resulted in even greater losses than usual, perhaps 20 to 25 percent of the harvest. The depth of the economic crisis is illustrated by the difficulties encountered in supplying energy products to the domestic market and by food rationing in large cities despite the near-record harvest. Food shortages in the winter of 1990-91 necessitated a call for help from the West. Although this was a sign of increased concern for human welfare, it was also an acknowledgment of economic mismanagement, a clear admission of policy failure that would have been unthinkable in the past. For 1991, real NMP is expected to show a decline of 15 percent, with a disproportionate fall in investment of 45 percent. Inflation, already accelerating during 1990, is expected to reach triple-digit rates in 1991. This sorry state of affairs immediately raises questions about the reasons for accelerated disintegration and about the possible future of the Soviet Union.

Our aim in this paper is to provide some answers. Because the quality of the data is poor and the legal and administrative situation is confusing, we concentrate on the fundamental issues. We minimize quantitative evaluations based on recent data, and we avoid discussing the details of the many legal and institutional changes that have been proposed.

In Chapter 2, we discuss the ingredients that are essential for a reform plan with a chance of success. Because the task is colossal, any feasible plan will fall seriously short of what seems desirable. We are convinced, however, that a thousand small steps taken over a long time span will not be enough to turn the situation around. Drastic and comprehensive reforms will have to be implemented or the Soviet

2

Union will not achieve a steep growth path. The list of reforms that seem necessary is well known. We give particular emphasis to financial reform, privatization, and macroeconomic stabilization. Only with a reasonably developed financial sector can the allocative control of resources, the monitoring of financial credits, and the entries and exits of firms be decentralized and privatized. In addition, the privatization of land, real estate, and industrial property is required to motivate Soviet citizens and to promote them to capitalist status with full participation rights. Such privatization can be achieved most easily and quickly by giving away property rights. Finally, macroeconomic stabilization requires a fundamental fiscal reform for effective control of expenditure and revenues and the decoupling of monetary policy from deficit financing.

In Chapter 3, we analyze the present crisis, stressing the unsettling effect of competing reform plans and of the lack of implementation. Together, these increase uncertainty and incentives to hedge against the worst outcomes. Lack of clear targets and of enforcement or incentive systems, as well as a general breakdown of law and order have further reduced the already meager efficiency of the system. The fiscal deficit, and therefore the money supply, are out of control and, for lack of available goods, a large monetary overhang has developed. Capacity to tax away this overhang in one way or another seems to be lacking.

Chapter 4 concentrates on the constitutional conflict between the Union and the republics, a conflict that is fundamental for the future of the Soviet Union. Drawing on the literature on economic integration, we argue that the Soviet Union is not an optimal economic or monetary union and that some republics, in particular the Baltic Republics, would be economically better off outside the Soviet economic union. Furthermore, reforms appear much more manageable and less costly at the republic rather than the Union level.

In Chapter 5, we attempt to evaluate the macroeconomic and sectoral constraints on future growth in the Soviet Union. The key constraint is the need for foreign capital. A comparison with Eastern European countries reveals that foreign capital is not the crucial problem for them, but it is for the Soviet Union. If GDP per capita in the Soviet Union is currently around $2,000 (U.S. dollars are cited throughout the paper), as estimated by most experts, current income levels in member countries of the European Community (EC) are still more than a generation away for the Soviet Union, even with sizeable foreign-capital assistance. To do better would require foreign funds in amounts

3

likely to exceed the West's willingness to put its savings at risk.

The G-7 Summit in London in July 1991 recognized the Soviet need for foreign assistance but failed to make substantial financial commitments. It was agreed that assistance to the Soviet Union would include (1) granting special status in the International Monetary Fund and World Bank, (2) efforts to promote trade, and (3) intensified efforts by all international institutions to support reforms with advice and expertise, particularly with regard to price decontrol and privatization, food distribution, technical assistance in energy and nuclear safety, and the conversion of defence industries to civilian output.

Because the country will face a severe foreign-capital constraint, it needs to attach top priority to exploiting its export potential. We therefore look at two key sectors: agriculture and energy. Agriculture has received priority in the government's budget, with subsidies and allocations in excess of 10 percent of GDP. Nevertheless, and in spite of the ample land and manpower available, this sector is the largest importer. We argue that there is considerable scope for reducing imports and even for becoming a net exporter of agricultural products. The preconditions are privatization and price liberalization. Joint ventures with foreign partners would prove useful for the modernization of storage, processing, and distribution of food. For external trade, the West, and in particular the European Community (EC), can make a major contribution by opening up protected agricultural home markets to imports from the Soviet Union and from Eastern Europe in general. This would require a reform of the Common Agricultural Policy (CAP) and a reduction in agricultural production.

Energy is the major export earning sector the importance of which has increased by shifting trade with Eastern Europe to world market prices payable in hard currency. Yet, energy production is expected to decline in the future, and marginal cost is increasing. The real task is to reduce energy waste. This requires incentives for the installation of energy-saving equipment and rescaling of energy-intensive production sectors. The potential savings are enormous, for the Soviet Union uses at least twice as much energy per dollar of GDP as the United States and four times as much as Western Europe. Again, the task is Herculean, and foreign technical, financial, and marketing support is required.

In Chapter 6, we summarize our main policy conclusions.

2 THE ESSENTIAL ELEMENTS OF A VIABLE REFORM PLAN

The ultimate goal of the reform process in the Soviet Union is to create a democratic society with a successful economy. For some Eastern European countries, in particular, Czechoslovakia, Hungary, and Poland, reform also includes full reintegration into the political, cultural, and economic mainstream of Europe, with membership in the European Community in the not-too-distant future. For the Soviet Union, the problem is much more complex. It must first find a new constitution that transforms or dissolves overcentralized structures. It must redefine from scratch the Union's relations with its republics and with the outside world. Whereas Czechoslovakia, Hungary, and Poland have only to prepare for a return to the European family, no comparable model or goal exists for the Soviet Union.

In a fundamental sense, therefore, the Soviet Union is alone. The difficulty in devising a viable reform plan lies in finding a route that minimizes the distance to be travelled and the risks of a lapse into dictatorship or economic chaos. Many difficulties can be avoided if it is recognized that partial reform can be worse than no reform at all. Everything is ultimately linked, and a market economy is a single indivisible mechanism that will not work if any one of its essential elements is missing. All this suggests the need for comprehensive and immediate reform.

A certain sequence in the implementation of reforms is nevertheless unavoidable. Monopolies should be broken up and banks made independent before privatization. Prices must be liberalized simultaneously with, or prior to, more independent decisionmaking. Current-account transactions of the balance of payments should be liberalized simultaneously with, or prior to, capital transactions.

Any reform program requires both the dismantling of old structures and the creation of new ones. To destroy first and then create produces chaos in the interim, but creating always takes longer than destroying. An efficient administration that can create new structures and execute new laws in a new spirit is therefore crucial to the success of the entire reform process. The task will be enormous, because the legal and institutional structure of a centrally planned economy is wholly inappropriate for a market economy. Constitutional, civil, business, and social laws must all be adapted to a different economic and social

5

order, and the state itself must be subject to the rule of law. Only this can ensure lasting confidence in reform programs.

We shall describe briefly in this chapter the main sectors that must be reformed. Although there is by now a consensus on what these are, it is still useful to recall them and to indicate the main problems we must anticipate. A major danger is that of failing to reform as completely and as quickly as possible because of allegedly adverse social consequences. Olson (1982) makes the point that big leaps occur only after the destruction of an ossified and nonperforming system and before the reestablishment of rigid structures in a new system. An opportunity for such a leap exists now, between these "worst of times" and what may yet be "the best of times."

Price Reform

The need to free administered prices and eliminate subsidies is by now universally recognized. Price reform is the cornerstone of all internal reforms. Only market-determined prices provide the scarcity signals that allow an economy to work properly. If prices for a large set of goods remain fixed, for whatever reason, the other elements of the reform package will not make much sense. The negative experiences of Hungary and Poland before 1990 with systems neither planned nor market based support this thesis.

It is sometimes argued that the prices of certain goods should not be liberalized too soon, that is, so-called essential foodstuffs, housing, energy, and interest rates. It would be a mistake, however, to try to isolate these sectors from the impact of market forces. In every case, there are better ways to reach the same redistributive impact.

It is worth emphasizing here that price reform per se cannot cause inflation. Simultaneously eliminating subsidies and production taxes may result in a higher or lower price level, because some prices should go up (foodstuffs, rents), but others should go down (many tradeable industrial goods). It should also be self-evident that price reform does not produce the desired effect—relative prices that reflect scarcity—unless firms face "hard" budget constraints (the foremost proponent of this thesis is Kornai, 1980, 1990). Without this financial discipline, new investment projects cannot be properly appraised for profitability, and firms will be encouraged to compensate for price increases by raising wages, thus triggering an inflationary spiral. Effective financial discipline, however, requires bankruptcy legislation, and firms must not be able to bargain with their financial regulators.

6

Banking and Financial Reform

The need for fundamental reform of the entire financial system and especially of banking is also self-evident. Financial reform comprises an institutional reform—the separation of central banking from commercial banking and the creation of capital markets—and a redefinition of the roles of various economic actors. It also requires legal restrictions on the privileges of government. The banking sector must not be obliged to finance government deficits, and there must be rules for control of the money supply.

Banks will play a central role during and after the transition to a market economy. This role is enhanced by the virtual absence of the capital markets that, in developed market economies, provide an important alternative source of investment funds. A capital market will develop, but this takes time, even when the government actively contributes to creating such a market by issuing securities to finance its deficits. Privatization will necessarily create a market for stocks, but this will also take time, as experience has shown. During the early period, when the centrally planned system has been abandoned but financial markets do not yet exist, banks will be the only economic agents able to assure an efficient allocation of resources and to develop healthy monetary and financial instruments. Improvement of efficiency in banking is therefore crucial.

A banking reform should start with the establishment of a two-tier banking system, that is, with the creation of an autonomous central bank. To be effective engines of economic growth, the new commercial banks should be endowed with a competitive, decentralized, "universal" structure. Because it will take considerable time to develop a smoothly functioning capital market, an institutional alternative is needed to facilitate long-term financing and monitoring of firms. The experience in German-speaking countries suggests that universal banking—with its virtual absence of regulatory restrictions—served well the needs of the early stages of industrial development in those countries. The universal banking model also entails dangers, however, mainly in restricting competition. It should, therefore, be paired with unrestrained access to the domestic market by foreign banks (for a historical overview and a critical assessment of universal banking in Germany, see Steinherr and Huveneers, 1990).

The break with central planning should also be a break with the past in terms of balance sheets, so that the entire private sector can look forward and invest. In an ongoing market-based system, all economic actors must pay for their past mistakes, even go bankrupt if necessary. The introduction of an entirely new system, however, justifies a clearing of old debts to enable everyone to make a clean start. Financial reform should therefore be accompanied by a radical clean-up of all balance sheets (for a forceful exposition of this argument, see Brainard, 1991). All intercompany debts and bank loans should be written down to zero, a relatively easy step at the beginning of the reform process, because all banks and firms are still the property of the state. Debt cancellation is therefore only a transfer among government agencies and has no net fiscal implications.

Although total debt cancellation would eliminate most of the assets of the banking system, the liabilities in the form of retail deposits would remain. This highlights a fact that is often overlooked. In a system that has only two sectors—the government (which owns the banking system and the corporate sector) and households—the *net* debt of the government consists of the money supply. Debt cancellation would bring this to the surface because the government would have to give the banks compensatory claims, that is, bonds that would carry a market rate of interest to match their deposit liabilities and net worth sufficient to reach a minimum gearing ratio.[1]

Fiscal Reform and Macroeconomic Stabilization

The need for fundamental fiscal reform becomes apparent if one considers that levies on firms have been the main sources of finance for the government under the old system. The introduction of the usual direct and indirect taxes will therefore completely change the structure of income and expenditure in the public sector. Moreover, direct control of firms has to be replaced with indirect controls (taxes, interest rates, etc.). Privatization will have another major repercussion

---

[1] There are other ways to deal with the weak balance sheet of the banking system and the overindebtedness of some firms. Brainard (1991) has proposed that bad debts be transferred from the banks' balance sheets to a new financial institution. This institution would exist only as long as necessary to wind down its portfolio of bad debts. This solution, as well as others, however, relies on a mechanism that distinguishes bad from good debts and that forces solvent firms to fulfil their obligations. It may be impossible to separate the wheat from the chaff, because that would require an efficient and honest administrative organization capable of auditing thousands of first-time balance sheets drawn up in a very unstable environment. Moreover, the process of deciding which firms should be forced to fulfil their obligations would be open to political interference. It would also weaken the incentive to restructure as quickly as possible, for firms making a profit too quickly would have to repay their debt.

8

on government finances: governments will receive higher tax revenues after the necessary tax reform and will pay out reduced subsidies. They will, however, no longer receive profits from privatized firms.

Fiscal and monetary policy are intimately related, for monetary policy can serve to finance fiscal deficits. A truly independent central bank, in charge of monetary policy and of regulating banks and financial markets, could, in principle, achieve sustained price stability. Given the financial pressures on the government, however, the central bank is not likely to win effective independence. In the very short run, the public sector has no alternative to monetary financing, and reforms may seriously destabilize fiscal revenues, at least until revised tax laws succeed in enlarging the tax base. With time, as growth resumes and the new tax system becomes fully operative, such transitory deficits will disappear. Deficits of this nature can therefore be seen as specific to the once-and-for-all regime change, and a unique financing method would be justified. For example, the government should consider selling housing and land to citizens, with payments spread out over the years, as with mortgage financing. To encourage sizeable down payments, a revisable positive real interest rate could be imposed. Such a program could be implemented rapidly without great difficulty and on a scale sufficient to stabilize the initial budget (this is an important element of the so-called Shatalin Plan; see Commission of the European Communities, 1990c).

To achieve some degree of price stability during the transition, a number of measures must thus be taken. First, the monetary overhang, if one exists, must be absorbed. The only way to achieve this is through a sale of state-owned assets, such as real estate, or through a currency reform. Blocking savings and other deposits does not solve the problem; it just buys time. Second, the budget deficit must be limited to the amount that can be financed by sales of bonds. Third, wage indexation has to be limited.

Radical measures are appropriate for macroeconomic stabilization when dangers appear on several fronts and when alternatives take too much time. A currency reform to reduce considerably the value of existing balances should therefore be considered. It would eliminate the monetary overhang with absolute certainty and would also reduce or eliminate a major drain on the budget, namely, interest payments on the government debt (which, as argued above, is equal to the money supply, that is, cash plus bank deposits of households). Moreover, it would also provide an occasion to suspend all backward-looking indexation mechanisms. It is often argued that a currency reform is unjust

9

because its incidence depends on the distribution of money—mainly savings deposits—among households. If most of these deposits represent a monetary overhang, however, they have probably been accumulated by those with higher incomes under the defunct and corrupt system.

Privatization

It is now increasingly accepted that privatization is an economic as well as a political choice. Economic democracy exercised through private ownership is a way to provide incentives to control resource allocation and the distribution of revenues. Privatization is therefore the central issue in the current reforms in the Soviet Union and Eastern Europe. These economies cannot operate on market principles without the incentives provided by private ownership. It is not easy, however, to reestablish quickly the private ownership of productive capital (see Tirole, 1991).

There are, basically, two ways to privatize. One is to sell ownership to nationals and foreigners and another is to distribute free ownership to citizens. Either approach allows variations in details, or the two can be combined. A combined approach seems to have been chosen in Czechoslovakia and Poland. Hungary thus far favors selling state assets, as discussions in the Soviet Union suggest it will also. We are convinced that, on balance, the arguments tip in favor of free distribution of ownership (see Gros and Steinherr, 1991).

It is possible to privatize housing and land quickly because their value can be determined fairly easily, and there is relatively little concern about foreigners or small groups achieving control over them. There is considerable hesitation, however, about the ways and means to privatize industrial firms (the service sector—smaller firms such as shops and hotels—which was neglected under central planning, can be privatized more quickly). The major problems perceived in current discussions are difficulties in properly valuing corporate assets, a dearth of domestic buyers with adequate financial resources, fear of "carpet-bagging" by foreigners, and the absence of an organized stock market.

It seems possible to circumvent all the perceived difficulties and, moreover, to achieve considerably more social justice through free distribution than through normal selling procedures. After all, the citizens of the socialist countries are supposedly the real owners of all national resources, which have been managed on their behalf by the state. The fact that state management has not been very efficient should not be a reason to deprive citizens of the little that is left. To the extent that there has been an (imposed) social contract, moreover,

10

each citizen in such so-called egalitarian societies has an implicit claim to accumulated social wealth, and all such claims should be the same. These rules of the past may not have been taken seriously, but they are the only logical rules there are if sense is to be read into a nonsense system—and they yield a rule for privatization.[2]

The basic idea is quite simple. Whenever one of the large public-sector companies is to be privatized, its capital should be divided into a number of shares and given away by the government. The shares could go to all citizens (individually or through a trust) or just to the workers of the firm.

Under the first alternative, each citizen would receive one share in the form of a book entry. Over time, as privatization progressed, each citizen would thus hold an increasingly diversified portfolio. Obviously, not all citizens would be interested in holding all shares received, and an informal market would therefore be established quickly. This would provide the basis for an over-the-counter market and eventually for an organized stock exchange. Any investor wishing to obtain control over a company would then have to acquire shares at market prices or with a takeover proposal. Whether the investor should be a resident would then be a question of secondary importance and would be decided by citizens acting as shareholders. A sale to foreigners could not be criticized, because it would not be a decision of an old or new *nomenklatura*.

Such a privatization program would be flexible enough to accommodate worker participation, if desired, by combining it with the second alternative. Workers could be allocated some of the shares of their firm, exercise their votes thereafter, and benefit from the firm's results. They should not be prevented in any way from disposing of such shares to achieve better risk diversification.

Such a rule for privatization offers several attractive advantages. First, as argued earlier, it would be consistent with social justice. Second, the starting point for the new capitalist society would be the point at which social capital is distributed equally. Capitalism would then be perceived as a system with the potential not only for greater dynamism but also for greater social justice than the defunct system of social ownership. Third, private ownership, when widely distributed at

[2] See Gros and Steinherr (1991) for more details. Blanchard et al. (1991) contains essentially the same ideas. Alternative approaches are analyzed by Dornbusch (1990). A precondition for any privatization scheme is, of course, the splitting up of state trusts and the establishment of a legal and regulatory framework that includes bankruptcy laws, company laws, and so forth (Cooter, 1991; Willig, 1991).

the starting point, should gain larger support than alternative property-right proposals. Fourth, no prior assessment of the value of the firm would be necessary. This job would be taken over at a subsequent stage by the stock exchange.

A major objection to this solution is that governments would have to forego revenues that would be generated by selling state firms. It seems doubtful, however, that the revenues foregone would be large. Any sales program of state-controlled assets would have to be distributed over several years, during which the state would continue to manage most of the firms. In Greece and Portugal, the entire stock-market capitalization is equal to 8 and 14 percent respectively of GDP. The potential privatization proceeds would not likely be even this large in the Soviet Union and the Eastern European countries, because the existing capital stock will often be close to worthless at the new price structure that will emerge. Even if amounts as high as 14 percent were realized, however, a privatization program spread over about a decade would not be likely to bring in revenues much larger than 1 percent of GDP per year.

External Aspects

Accepting foreign competition and the idea of the international division of labor is arguably the only way to catch up with Western standards of living. The Soviet Union needs to open its economy to international trade and to have access to the huge market on its doorstep: the European Community (EC), or rather, the European economic space that also encompasses the European Free Trade Association (EFTA).

The problem of excess demand for foreign goods, paired with scarce foreign-exchange reserves, can be dealt with through tariffs. To minimize distortions of domestic resource allocations, a uniform tariff of between, say, 10 and 30 percent initially should be adopted. This would allow domestic producers to compete with imports on domestic markets, even if their costs are substantially higher. Admittedly, tariff protection is only a second-best solution to the excess demand for foreign goods. At a more fundamental level, this excess demand can only come about because the excess consumption of some agents is not financed by private capital flows, but by the central bank, that is, the exchange rate is overvalued. The appropriate first-best answer to an excess demand for foreign goods is therefore devaluation. A tariff might also be justified, however, because of the revenue it would yield at a time when tax revenues will be very difficult to collect.

Opening up economies to international trade will also partly solve another problem. Even after the reforms, many firms will be the only domestic suppliers of certain products. With strong international competition, domestic monopolists will not be able to use their monopoly power to charge prices higher than the world market level (see Lipton and Sachs, 1990).

Full integration into the world trading system requires a convertible currency.[3] Although current-account convertibility would be a viable solution, complete convertibility is certainly preferable over the long run because it represents a binding constraint for macroeconomic management. The stringency of this constraint can, however, be modulated by the exchange-rate arrangement adopted and by complementary policy measures such as tariff protection, as mentioned above.[4]

The degree of flexibility for the exchange rate becomes a crucial decision once at least current-account convertibility has been established. The free-floating option has gained little support. If the Soviet Union wants to initiate a process of economic integration with Western economies, raise external trade, and attract foreign investment, it must guarantee stability, among other conditions, and it must reduce uncertainties about the exchange rate. A fixed but adjustable exchange rate is therefore the only alternative, but it must be supported by capital controls, if the exchange-rate commitment is not to be undermined by speculative flows resulting from political uncertainties during the transition.

An intermediate regime between fixed and flexible rates, that is, a dual-rate system, might be the best solution. It would be economically equivalent to a fixed exchange rate with variable capital controls. In such a system, current-account transactions can be conducted at the fixed exchange rate, while financial funds flow in and out of the country at a

---

[3] A currency is fully convertible if it can be traded against other currencies without restrictions or justifications. In most countries, convertibility is restricted according to the nature of the transaction (current account, capital account, or specific transactions within each), the identity of the agent (domestic or foreign, specialized agencies, trading firms, or individuals), or the amounts involved.

[4] We do not discuss here transitional arrangements for increased convertibility between Eastern European countries and the Soviet Union. For a discussion of the desirability of a transitional Eastern European Payments Union (EEPU), see Bofinger (1990), Kenen (1991), and Steinherr et al. (1990). These authors stress the limited usefulness of such a union because trade within this group accounts for only a small fraction of their potential overall trade. Beyond the immediate need of preventing a total collapse of trade, fostering trade inside this group of countries is therefore less important than eliminating impediments to trade with the rest of the world by a rapid return to at least partial current-account convertibility.

freely flexible exchange rate. This is, in fact, the current system in Poland.

The underlying aim of a dual-rate system is to shelter the domestic real economy from external and domestic financial shocks. In effect, the burden of adjustment to financial shocks is redirected from the domestic interest rate to the financial exchange rate. The current-account exchange rate can be kept fixed, thereby maintaining a welcome stability for the relative prices of goods and services.

In fact, by imposing a variable tax on capital transactions (equal to the flexible gap between the controlled and uncontrolled exchange rates), a dual-rate system reduces the substitutability between domestic and external assets without erecting any barrier to capital flows. This imperfect substitutability confers some latitude on the domestic monetary authorities. The spread between the controlled and the uncontrolled rates is limited, however, by the impossibility of a leak-proof separation between the two exchange-market compartments.[5]

A regime of this sort, however, should be strictly temporary. Given the flexibility inherent in a dual-rate system, moreover, it would be easy to eliminate gradually the implicit capital controls through a commitment to keep the spread between the two exchange rates within certain limits reduced over time.

---

[5] For an analysis of the effects of arbitrage between the two exchange markets, see Gros (1988).

3 THE PRESENT CRISIS IN THE SOVIET UNION

We now turn to a description of the present situation in the Soviet Union. Our purpose is not to provide a detailed account of the economic chaos that is developing, but to show how this situation arises from inconsistencies in the policies pursued so far.

At present (July 1991) none of the essential components of reform discussed in the previous chapter has been implemented. There has been no (1) *price reform*: prices for some goods were increased in the spring of 1991, but these prices were not liberalized, and some increases were subsequently rescinded; (2) *banking reform*: a banking reform has existed on paper since November 1990, but it has not been implemented; (3) *fiscal reform*: because there has been no fiscal reform, there has been no macroeconomic stabilization, despite the attempt to reduce the money supply by confiscating banknotes of higher denominations; (4) *privatization*: privatization has not advanced, except in the sense that managers of state-owned enterprises have gained more independence; or (5) *exchange reform*: on the external side, the foreign-trade monopolies of various government institutions have not been abolished officially, and the system of multiple exchange rates has, if anything, became even more complicated, along with other regulations regarding foreign direct investment.

The main reason for this sorry state of affairs is that the old planning system is no longer strictly enforced, yet a market economy cannot emerge because no reforms have been implemented. The first section of this chapter is based on the Commission of European Communities report on "Stabilization, Liberalization, and Devolution . . . in the Soviet Union" (Commission, 1990c, chap. 5) and provides a brief overview of the failed reform attempts of 1990-91. The second section discusses the macroeconomic destabilization, and the third describes briefly the regional disintegration that has followed.

Competing, but not Implemented, Reform Plans

Reform projects have a long tradition in the Soviet economy. Because the system of central planning has never worked satisfactorily, it has been overhauled from time to time—since World War II, in 1957, 1965, and 1979. None of the reforms, however, was supposed to change the nature of the system. Similarly, the various mini-reforms

15

attempted between 1985 and 1989 were also directed at increasing the efficiency of the existing system of central planning. The only significant trace from this period is the law on cooperatives of 1988, which allowed a small private sector to emerge in services.

The partial and piecemeal reforms up to 1989 undermined the central planning system and thus led to a deterioration of the economic situation. This, in turn, led in 1989-90 to the general admission that the entire system of central planning had to be abandoned. During the summer of 1990, three competing comprehensive reform plans for the transition to a market economy were presented to the Supreme Soviet, which was to adopt the necessary legislation. The Supreme Soviet, however, refused to approve any of the three plans; instead, it gave President Gorbachev broad emergency powers and authorized him to present a plan of his own. The compromise plan presented by the president, called "Basic Guidelines for the Stabilization of the National Economy and the Transition to a Market Economy" was then approved by a large majority on October 19, 1990.

The president's guidelines, which are more general and political than the other three plans, became the official program of the Union government, but their implementation was checked by the constitutional crisis that developed between the Union and the republics.[1] In May 1991, the Union government presented again a vague outline of a reform plan, concentrating on macroeconomic stabilization.

The four major plans that dominated the discussion in 1990 all agreed on three final goals: a market economy, stabilization of the economy, and the preservation of at least an economic and monetary union for the territory of the Soviet Union. Furthermore, all of these plans contained most of the necessary elements outlined above.

But there are important differences between the reform plans in the emphasis given to these goals and the speed with which they should be attained. In general, the government programs put more emphasis on macroeconomic stabilization than on liberalization, and they insist for obvious reasons on more powers for the Union.

The famous "500 days program" elaborated for the Russian government by a group under Professor Shatalin came closest to containing all the elements enumerated above and discussed in Chapter 2. Although 500 days represent a rather protracted "big bang," this long transition

---

[1] A law establishing a two-tier banking system and an independent central bank was also approved and was supposed to become effective by November 1, 1990, but it has so far remained on paper.

16

period might be considered as ambitious in view of the enormous number of measures that would have to be taken.

None of these programs could be implemented, however, as long as there persisted the "war of laws," under which each republic passed a declaration of sovereignty stating that its laws would take precedence over Union law, whereas the Union government insisted that Union law would take precedence. The implementation of reforms can come only after an agreement is reached with most republics on a new Union treaty that defines the powers of the republics and the Union. The agreement reached in May 1991 may provide a basis for such a treaty, but it is so vague that its importance is impossible to assess.

The prospects for a speedy implementation of a comprehensive reform package are slim not only because the political balance of power continues to shift. A reform package must be translated into thousands of laws and regulations, which then have to be applied by the bureaucracy. For political reasons, it will not be possible for the Soviet Union simply to import legislation from abroad. Just drafting and approving all the necessary new legislation (and repealing all the old legislation) will take some time. To transform the old bureaucracy so that it will implement these laws in the new spirit will also require time.

Yet, the macroeconomic destabilization that is taking place in the absence of a credible reform program demonstrates that the present situation is not tenable in the long run. This economic chaos might therefore be the decisive factor leading finally to implementation of some reforms.

Macroeconomic Destabilization

As suggested by official Soviet data and confirmed by studies of the International Monetary Fund et al. (1991) and Commission of the European Communities (1990c), growth of the Soviet economy has been declining since the end of the 1950s. Although the statistical data cannot be considered fully reliable, it is certain that this decline has recently accelerated sharply. Why?

The simple answer is that the Soviet Union had a system of incentives and controls and of fixing objectives that, although not efficient, worked. When the system itself was put into question, the incentive and command structure began to disintegrate, which produced all-the-more negative effects because the system was excessively centralized. This process of disintegration was further accelerated by the increased uncertainty created when profound systemic changes were expected but repeatedly delayed.

17

Expectations of liberalization or of a regime change have also allowed, for the first time in a lifetime, the manifestation of disagreement and the open assertion of conflict. Malfunctioning of the Soviet economy was always to some extent due to lack of motivation and to passivity in work commitment. This passivity has increased and become more open and more pronounced. Strikes are not only (and not even mainly) motivated by higher wage claims; they pursue, first of all, political demands for some sort of reform—a decentralization of power, greater individual freedom, and so on.[2] What is often treated as "sabotage" is simply a move away from a strict enforcement system to one of less control and greater individual responsibility. Such a transition phase is necessarily disorganized, contradictory, and bad for production levels. Particularly worrisome in the Soviet case is the extent of disagreement on all levels and the fact that the old regime structures—the Party, the KGB, and the military-industrial complex—have kept enough power to block or even overturn reforms. Progress in liberalization is therefore protracted and never more than a complicated compromise. Protraction nurtures the risk of complete destabilization and of hyperinflation, and the extent to which compromises must be accepted makes even the long-term gains appear doubtful.

In the past, the implementation of centralized planning was generally monitored through the Communist Party's widespread influence within the hierarchy of state enterprises. The loss by the Party and its organs of unchallenged leadership, the rejection of planning objectives, and the greater independence granted to plant managers have all resulted in serious dysfunctions. Planning has increasingly taken place in a bureaucratic ivory tower, cut off from an economic reality that belies official statistics. Enforcement mechanisms for plan targets have disappeared with the waning influence of Party directors in enterprises. Managers have been granted greater independence to achieve what? Surely not to plan goals, but to plan, in fact, their own survival and benefit. This has had several consequences: loss of supply for the official circuits and greater recourse to barter trade, and reduced transfers to government agencies and augmented internal uses by firms of any surpluses. One use, in particular, has consisted in granting workers' demands for increased income. This microeconomic behavior has rendered inflation control much more difficult, as there are no effective constraints on wage demands. Hence, the overall effect of

---

[2] The recent law prohibiting strikes in key industries and strikes motivated by political aims is an "emergency measure" pointing in the wrong direction.

reduced controls and lack of appropriate incentives has been that production has declined, the flow of goods reaching the shops has declined even more rapidly, state revenues have declined, and inflation has increased.

This process has been made worse by the expectations of reforms and, in particular, of price liberalization (or of price increases). These expectations have produced hoarding, further motivated by the lack of appropriate financial instruments. Speculative hoarding has increased excess demand and raised black-market prices. Price liberalization will also require a devaluation of the domestic currency, and this expectation will increase the flight into foreign currency. Demand for foreign goods will also increase as a result of rising excess domestic demand and the expectation of the future devaluation. The trade deficit will increase as controls, never perfect, become even less effective than usual in this period of defunct law and order. Thus, a major cause of destabilization is the *delay* in taking reform decisions—which are, however, discussed endlessly.[3]

Several presidential decrees since December 1990 have aimed at reestablishing central planning by restoring the lost authority of Gosplan (the state planning agency) and banning barter deals between enterprises. Lacking macroeconomic policy instruments for the stabilization of the economy, the central authorities have reverted to reliance on the Party, the KGB, and the military complex. But, short of using force to counter the disintegration of the central political authority, going back to the old Communist system seems impossible.

In the past, the Soviet Union had no autonomous monetary policy. The growth of the money supply was directly determined by the fiscal deficit. Control of fiscal policy was therefore of paramount importance. With the loss of control over enterprises, the tax base has been substantially eroded, and the conflict between the republics and the Union over the ownership of enterprises and the new fiscal structure of the Union poses serious additional problems. At stake is how much revenue the republics will remit to the central authorities and in what form. In 1990, the republics contributed 55 percent of the central government budget revenue and accounted for about 51 percent of the central government budget expenditure. The republics would like to reduce their contributions considerably.

Another budgetary uncertainty is created by price reforms. In April

---

[3] An excellent theoretical analysis of the effects of expected reform measures is provided by Calvo and Frenkel (1991).

1991, retail prices were raised, increasing the general price level by some 60 to 70 percent. This may allow a reduction in state subsidies, but the net budgetary effect is uncertain. In particular, partial compensation for the price increase is to be granted and a one-time 40-percent compensatory increase given on all individual savings accounts. If this is done, the inflationary spiral will start to move, and it will not stop until the real value of the money supply is drastically reduced either through further price increases without compensation or through a currency reform.

The uncontrolled budget situation—and the monetization of deficits—represents an obvious destabilizing influence on the inflation rate and on economic activity in general. The continuing lack of wage and fiscal control is a classroom example of the way to cause hyperinflation. The expectation of hyperinflation is, by itself, likely to have serious repercussions on economic activity. In a desperate attempt to control the budgetary explosion, the government has taken the easiest course politically and cut back investment expenditure. Investment tumbled by 3 percent in 1989, by 25 percent in 1990, and is forecast to fall by 45 percent in 1991.

The administration is now unable to make the difficult choices necessary to stem destabilization. At best, it carries out crisis management. The declining availability of resources pits groups in society and in different parts of the administration against each other in a fierce fight for power and resources—Union vs. republics, military vs. civilian, industry vs. agriculture, the various industrial sectors vs. themselves, and so forth.

Enterprises are faced with serious financial difficulties in this process, because the credit mechanism is not adapted to rapid changes in domestic and foreign prices. Thus, even fundamentally sound firms may be forced out of business for lack of payments or credit lines. In particular, the absence of foreign-trade credit represents a serious bias against exportation. The breakdown of foreign-exchange allocations makes it very difficult to maintain traditional import patterns. Because the Soviet structure of production is highly specialized and lacks a sufficient elasticity of substitution, import cuts create bottlenecks, stop domestic production, and feed back into reduced exports. These difficulties illustrate vividly the point made in Chapter 2 that financial reforms are among the most urgent needed.

In addition to the general problem of reforming defunct economic structures, halting the decline in production, and returning the economy to a growth path, Soviet policymakers are under serious pressure to deal rapidly with growing financial and foreign-trade imbalances.

Monetary destabilization. During 1990, total money income rose by about 17 percent, although production declined. Retail prices increased by 5 percent, but the underlying rate of inflation, including the suppressed component officially estimated at about 20 percent for 1990, is expected to exceed 100 percent in 1991.

The causes of accelerating inflation are three: a monetary overhang, monetization of the budget deficit, and wage push. Policies are needed to deal with all three causes simultaneously.

Long queues everywhere and the large-scale rationing introduced for the winter of 1990-91 are already *prima facie* evidence of a large monetary overhang. The collapse of the distribution system is certainly also a factor, but, whatever the state of the distribution system, the queues show that, at the current price level, the public wishes to run down its money holdings through purchases.

Although the monetary statistics available do not suggest a particularly large overhang, they are not very reliable.[4] Cash in circulation is said to have exceeded R 150 billion in 1990, and the amount is increasing rapidly. The sum of all monetary assets held by households, mainly in savings deposits and cash, is estimated to total between R 600 to 750 billion. With GDP estimated officially at R 1,000 billion, the cash-to-GDP ratio can be put at above 15 percent and the money-to-GDP ratio at about 60 to 75 percent. The cash-to-GDP ratio is higher than in the poorer Western European countries (for example, Portugal and Greece), where it is about 10 percent. This indicator alone would suggest an increase in the price level of "only" 50 percent, but, once the public expects such an increase for the near future, the equilibrium cash-to-GDP ratio will sink to the values of about 5 percent that can be found in Latin America. Because there are no other financial instruments available, it is not possible to say whether or not the current holdings of savings deposits represent an equilibrium.

There are three basic policy options for reducing a monetary overhang: an increase of the price level to reduce the real money supply to the level of demand, a currency reform to reduce the excess supply, or an increase in real interest rates to increase the desired level of demand

---

[4] In particular, due to a virtual automaticity of interfirm trade credits and the availability of administrative credit lines, cash requirements of institutions, unlike those of individuals, are much smaller than in the West. The IMF et al.(1991) estimates excess liquidity at R 250 billion, or two-thirds of financial assets. In 1990, this was estimated at about 70 percent of GDP, compared to 50 percent in 1986.

for financial assets. All three are forms of taxation and differ only in their tax incidence. We prefer a currency reform, because it cannot put an inflationary spiral into motion and because it can achieve the desired effect overnight.

The second source of inflation, monetary financing of the fiscal deficit, will operate even after the monetary overhang has been eliminated and can therefore lead to prolonged periods of high inflation. This source of inflation is therefore much more important in the long run.

At present, the Union budget deficit is expected to reach about 10 to 15 percent of output in 1991 unless some drastic action is taken. Given that most politicians, and the Supreme Soviet, constantly emphasize the need to cushion the impact of price reform on the income of many social groups, this deficit is not likely to shrink soon. The experience in many developing countries suggests that the inflation tax rarely yields more than 3 percent of GDP, so a deficit of 10 to 15 percent could easily lead to hyperinflation. The independence of the central bank that was written into law will, in these circumstances, fail to materialize.

It is too early to tell whether the third inflationary factor, widespread wage indexation, will be realized. Indexation is foreseen by most reform plans, and the first substantial increase in prices was partly offset by wage increases. If real wages (at measured prices) are not allowed to fall, hyperinflation must be the result. Moreover, as long as enterprises are not subjected to a hard budget constraint, there is no real restraint on wage demands. Hence, the wage increases of 1990 and 1991 do not augur well.

Foreign-trade imbalances. The external accounts of the Soviet Union were roughly balanced until 1989, when it had for the first time a current-account deficit (in convertible currency) of $5.9 billion. Imports were scaled back in 1990 to stem the deficit, and, although the volume of exports is estimated to have declined by 6 percent, an improvement in the terms of trade, due partly to higher oil prices, raised the value of exports by 5 percent (see Table 1).

In 1990, the trade balance in nonconvertible currencies deteriorated sharply to reach a deficit of $6 billion. The reductions in volume expected for 1991 are drastic: export volumes are forecast to decline by 64 percent and import volumes by 58 percent. With the terms of trade improving strongly following the reforms of the Council for Mutual Economic Assistance (CMEA), however, the net effect is likely to be a small surplus.

Partly to stem the flight into dollars and partly to redress the foreign-trade deficit, the ruble was devalued in November 1990 from a commercial rate of R 0.6 rubles per U.S. dollar to R 1.8. The significance for the trade account of this pronounced devaluation was reduced, however, by the rigidities of the foreign-trade administration and of internally administered prices.

Additional difficulties lie ahead. The Soviet Union benefited in 1990 from the sharp rise in oil prices, but these were reversed in 1991. Nevertheless, oil sales to Eastern Europe will benefit from applying world market prices and from payments in convertible currencies. In trade outside the CMEA, the terms of trade are expected to decline by over 8 percent. Domestic pressures to import foodstuffs and consumer goods remain strong, and the demand for capital goods can be scaled down only through drastic cuts in domestic investment. The prospects for securing convertible-currency payments from the former CMEA countries are also very uncertain. Soviet imports from the rest of

TABLE 1

THE SOVIET CURRENT-ACCOUNT BALANCE IN CONVERTIBLE-CURRENCY TRADE
(*in billions of U.S. dollars*)

	1988	1989	1990 [a]	1991 [b]
Trade balance	2.6	−2.2	−0.4	−1.0
Total exports	31.2	32.9	34.7	36.7
Petroleum	9.3	9.4	12.6	12.6
Military	7.8	7.2	5.0	4.0
Total imports	−28.5	−35.1	−35.1	−37.7
Agriculture	−6.0	−8.0	−9.9	−8.0
Balance on services,				
income, and transfers	−3.2	−3.7	−4.4	−1.6
Interest payments	−2.8	−3.7	−4.4	−4.7
Official transfers	0.0	0.0	0.8	3.4
Current-account balance	−0.6	−5.9	−4.8	−2.5
Total external debt	43.0	54.0	57.1	57.1
Nongold external reserves	15.3	14.2	8.5	7.9
Net debt	17.7	39.3	48.6	49.2
Monetary gold sales	n.a.	3.6	5.0	4.7
Memoranda:				
Export-volume change	6.3%	−1.0%	−5.9%	17.5%
Import-volume change	8.6%	18.5%	−5.0%	8.9%
Terms-of-trade change	−12.1%	2.7%	6.4%	−8.6%

SOURCE: Institute of International Finance, 1991.

[a] Estimated

[b] Forecast

Eastern Europe seem to have collapsed in the absence of arrangements for the financial clearing of these trade flows.

Foreign indebtedness. As a result of the current-account deficit emerging in 1989, the financial position of the Soviet Union has greatly deteriorated. For decades before 1989, the debt position of the Soviet Union was unassailably strong. Debt and ratios of relative indebtedness were low, and deposits in Western banks were maintained at very high levels. In addition, the country had massive stocks of nonmonetary gold, which could be used as a secondary reserve asset. During most of the 1980s, the private markets lent readily to the Soviet Union. The banks' unguaranteed share of Soviet debt rose from 25 percent in 1982 to 62 percent in 1988, while the officially guaranteed share declined from 67 percent to 32 percent. The Soviet Union thus became progressively more dependent on the willingness of private markets to provide credit. With the worsening of the current-account balance and the weakening of central control after 1988, the situation has rapidly worsened. Net debt rose from $28 billion in 1988 to $49 billion at the end of 1990.

Even with this rapid rise in debt, the Soviet Union is still only a moderately indebted country by most measures. If the debt increase were the only problem, the Soviet Union would not be in serious financial difficulties. This sharp rise in debt, however, has been accompanied by a virtual collapse of central control over international payments. In the past, all foreign-exchange payments were tightly regulated by the Gosbank (State Bank) and the Vneshekonombank (Bank for Foreign Economic Affairs), but this control has slipped badly in the last two years. Many independent banks and enterprises have begun to import or borrow overseas without the authorization, or even the knowledge, of the Vneshekonombank, which has not been able to monitor such transactions. As to the components of the rising overall debt, a sharp rise has occurred in short-term obligations, which are estimated to have increased from some $12 billion at the end of 1988 to $19 billion a year later. No doubt, bankers and suppliers believed that, by granting short-term trade-related credits, they were minimizing their own risks, but the end result has been to place extreme liquidity pressures on the Soviet Union. It has begun to fall behind in its payments, and these arrears are accumulating. External reserves, excluding gold, declined from $15 billion in 1989 to $8 billion in 1991.

With growing awareness of the chaotic economic conditions in the country and the payments arrears, private financial institutions have become wary of lending to the Soviet Union. Net lending peaked in 1989 at more than $8 billion but turned negative in 1990 by $11.7

billion and is expected to remain negative in 1991 at about $6.7 billion. The Soviet Union now faces a liquidity crisis.

Because Western banks are unwilling to lend to the Soviet Union without guarantees from Western governments, the large financial resources needed to rebuild the Soviet Union are not likely to be forthcoming. A small share of these will be covered by Western official sources, but a different *structure d'accueil* will be essential to attract private capital—that is, proper legal and market frameworks in a totally reformed Soviet Union.

A further worrying sign is the discrepancy that exists between the data on the current account and the increase in *net* foreign debt. From 1988 to 1990, net debt increased by $21 billion and monetary gold sales (the known part of overall gold sales) amounted to $8.6 billion. Of these approximately $30 billion, only $11 billion were used to finance accumulated current-account deficits; an explanation is thus needed for the remaining $19 billion.

A substantial part of the remainder might be accounted for by capital flight, largely in the accumulation of dollar and deutsche mark bank notes through the black market. Enterprises may also have been tempted to hide some of their foreign-exchange earnings, but it is not clear how they could have done so, for foreign exchange is still centrally administered. This flight of capital indicates that the public does not believe the government will succeed in stabilizing the economy. An increasing degree of "dollarization," however, can make stabilization even more difficult.

Regional Disintegration

The Soviet Union consists at present of fifteen "sovereign" republics, twenty "autonomous republics" (in the territories of the federated republics of Russia, Georgia, and Azerbaijan), and varying degrees of subdivisions within all the republics into entities such as autonomous territories and regions, autonomous regions within territories, and autonomous districts. All of these subdivisions have their own competences, but these have been practically irrelevant in the past, because the Communist Party has ensured that there was a strict line of command from top to bottom of the system.

The situation changed rapidly with the perestroika movement initiated by Gorbachev. The first multicandidate elections at the republican and other regional levels brought many noncommunists into office, and the inconsistencies and legal uncertainties of the old constitutional system are therefore coming out into the open. It should be noted, in this regard, that there is no accepted constitutional court to decide jurisdictional disputes.

In the power struggle between different levels of governments, the republics, with developed administrative structures, have generally emerged as the only viable alternative to the Union government. The lower levels are not at present viable autonomous units. Moreover, the republican level is the only level that can generally appeal to nationalist sentiments, for most republics (including the Ukraine, Belorussia, and the Transcaucasian republics) had brief periods of independence during the civil war that followed the 1917 revolution. All the republics except one have declared their sovereignty and insist on the supremacy of republican law over Union law (contrary to the Union constitution). Despite some spectacular actions by other regional authorities, most of the economic splitting off is therefore taking place along republican lines.

Some republics have already established customs at their borders, although they cannot yet enforce controls; others have imposed restrictions on the use of the ruble; and several plan to introduce their own currencies. Many bilateral trade agreements have been negotiated, usually involving the barter of goods that are no longer available through the official system. The ruble has thus stopped functioning effectively as money in the face of accelerating inflation and the absence of functioning markets.

On November 1, 1990, a currency reform was introduced in the Ukraine, with some of the tax effects necessary to be effective. To buy anything, Ukrainians have to pay with rubles and government coupons of equal value. Moreover, when workers collect wages, they are given coupons equal to 70 percent of the rubles they receive, The coupon system thus cuts expenditure from wages by 30 percent. Savings have been frozen, as there is no matching stock of coupons. The reform thus treats flows (wages) differently from stocks (savings), as we suggested in an earlier discussion (Gros and Steinherr, 1990), and uses coupons to end the ruble's legal-tender privilege. An immediate result of this reform is that goods have returned to the shops. Although the coupon system was introduced as a temporary measure, it is likely to stay. It obviously discourages exports (which earn rubles without coupons) and encourages imports (the only goods obtainable for rubles alone). This system is thus equivalent to a 30-percent revaluation of the ruble for Ukrainians, at least at the retail level. The Russian and Belorussian governments are studying similar schemes. If they adopt them, the Soviet Union will be broken up in economic terms while still retaining a common currency *pro forma*, and without border controls by republics.

Uncoordinated attempts by individual republics to introduce their own currencies have a serious external effect, however, because they intensify the monetary overhang in the rest of the Union. Some coordination in the breakup of the ruble area is therefore necessary. If this coordination is not forthcoming, each republican government will have a strong incentive to repudiate the public debt implicit in the money balances held by households. The Russian government, which will probably be the last to keep the ruble, might have then to deal with the monetary overhang of the entire Union.

4 ECONOMIC COSTS AND BENEFITS OF REGIONAL DISINTEGRATION

We have shown in Chapter 3 that the increasing regional disintegration was the main reason why the 1990 reform plans were not implemented. Moreover, the loss of control by the Union government over the budgets of the republics has been an important cause of the large public-sector deficit that makes macroeconomic stabilization impossible for the time being. The process of regional disintegration has thus been very damaging to the economy of the Soviet Union. Many Western observers and the Union government have therefore argued that a disintegration of the Soviet Union into a number of independent economic units competing against each other should be avoided as much as possible, even in the face of demands by some republics for total independence. The purpose of this chapter, therefore, is to analyze from a purely economic point of view whether it is indeed advisable to keep the Soviet Union together, that is, whether the economic and monetary union the Soviet Union still represents should be preserved.

As discussed above, we take the existing republics of the Soviet Union as the natural lower-level economic units, because the administrative and political structures necessary to create the institutional and legal framework required for the functioning of a market economy exist only at the republican level. Moreover, most republics (except Russia) are economic regions as homogenous as most European countries.

We start with the issue that dominates the present political agenda, namely, whether a centralized approach to reform is preferable to competition in reform among the individual republics. We turn next to the lessons that can be drawn from the literature on fiscal federalism and then to the importance of the "Soviet common market," that is, the costs and benefits for any individual republic of participating in a Soviet customs union. Finally, we discuss the incentives for individual republics to keep the ruble as their currency.

The division adopted in this chapter is artificial in that a republic that secedes would, for political reasons, want to leave the Soviet economic sphere in all of its aspects. But it is still useful to analyze the economic factors that explain why some republics want to implement their own reform plans, conduct their own fiscal and commercial policies, and introduce their own currencies.

28

Centralization or Competition in Reform?

The Union-republic controversy has undoubtedly delayed the implementation of fundamental reforms, but this does not necessarily imply that a centralized reform plan is the best option. Fundamentally, the issue is the following: there is at present a vast economic area with completely distorted prices and without the legal and institutional framework necessary for a market economy. Can any subunit of this area gain by implementing reforms on its own and thus allowing its inhabitants to trade freely at true market prices? In general, the answer should be yes.

It is often alleged that price reform has to be implemented at the Union level because differences in prices would lead consumers to buy where the goods are cheapest. As long as the ruble remains the common currency of the Soviet Union and there are no restrictions on inter-republican trade, price reform in one republic alone would indeed make it profitable to arbitrage price differences. This arbitrage is the essence of a market economy, however, and should thus not be viewed as a cost. If any republic were to implement most of the essential reforms outlined above, its price structure would be different from that of the rest of the Union. Residents of other republics would then certainly come to "plunder" its shops for goods cheaper in that particular republic. But this "plunder" would in reality be advantageous, for the goods involved would be sold at their marginal cost of production, and an increase in demand would lead to an increase in the profits of domestic producers.[1] Furthermore, consumers in the republic initiating a reform in isolation would gain by buying other goods from the rest of the Union at their old subsidized prices.

In reality, however, shops in the Soviet Union are now mostly empty. This implies that the impact of a radical reform on the supply of new goods and on the distribution system should be more important than the impact of changing the prices of the limited number of old goods actually available at their official rates. Entrepreneurs in a republic that was the first to implement fundamental reforms would therefore gain by being able to satisfy a Unionwide pent-up demand for diversified products.

The rest of the Union would lose from an uncoordinated reform process to the extent that the residents of a republic that initiates

---

[1] This argument holds under the assumption that the price reform was implemented together with the other structural reforms outlined in Chapter 2. See the section on a Soviet customs union below for an exception to the argument.

reforms on its own would then buy more Union goods at prices below cost. This is a consequence of the distorted Union price structure, however, and not a cost of an uncoordinated price reform. On the contrary, this effect is beneficial because it gives the rest of the Union an incentive to implement reforms.

In brief, the spillover effects of goods arbitrage that would arise from an uncoordinated reform process do not constitute a valid argument for a centralized reform process. Moreover, experience has shown that a credible reform strategy has to be adapted to specific local circumstances. Some competition to select the best way of creating a market economy should therefore be beneficial.

If there were a credible commitment at the Union level to implement a radical reform, the issue of a decentralized transition to a market economy would not even arise. There are reasons to believe, however, that the Union authorities may always be more cautious in their approach to reform than the authorities in the smaller republics.

The creation of a market economy should benefit all citizens in the long run. However, some groups are bound to lose initially, and it is even possible that the majority of the population will be made worse off for a limited period during which existing inefficient enterprises are being liquidated and new efficient ones created to take their place. This makes a fast transition difficult, because the authorities, who now have to obtain democratic approval for their actions, will try to shelter many groups from the adverse effects of the transition.[2] It is apparent that this problem increases with the degree of heterogeneity in the economy. This explains why the smaller republics, which are more homogenous regions, are generally willing to go faster and take more radical measures.[3]

Furthermore, the creation of a market economy is impossible without the support of an administration that executes and interprets the new laws in the new spirit (Gros and Steinherr, 1990; Sachs, 1990). It is

[2] Western societies have always had to face a similar problem, which is analyzed in the literature on the political economy of protection. Measures that will hurt a small group but benefit the rest of the economy may not be taken, even if the net gain to society is large. The resistance from the small group is well organized, whereas the support from the rest of the society is weak, because the gain for each individual agent is small.

[3] Differences in local attitudes toward the market economy are often used as excuses by politicians, but Shiller, Boycko, and Korobov (1991) have found a surprising degree of similarity in popular attitudes in the United States and the Soviet Union toward market mechanisms.

much easier to set up and control such an administration for a small Baltic state than for the entire Soviet Union, the total administrative body of which runs into the millions. The authorities of the smaller, and therefore more homogenous, republics have the additional advantage that action can be concentrated on a smaller number of important sectors (some republics need not deal with the issue of converting defense industries or with an energy sector that needs attention). This is an additional argument for allowing the republics to implement their own reforms.

Finally, the large military-industrial complex that dominates the economy of the Soviet Union represents a powerful obstacle to a radical reform that would necessarily diminish its power. Large expenses for military purposes serve only the interest of a Union concerned about its global role. Individual republics do not see the need to maintain a large military establishment and are therefore more likely to overcome its resistance to radical reform.

The above-mentioned arguments suggest that the implementation of reforms should also be left to the republics. Otherwise, reforms initiated by the republics may be blocked at the Union level. In the present legal and political framework, the bureaucracy of the Union, especially the KGB, can deter entrepreneurs from exploiting opportunities created by the laws of the republics. A new Union treaty to establish the rule of law and clear up some of the legal uncertainties seems therefore to be a precondition for an effective devolution of the reform process.

Fiscal Federalism

A central aspect of the power struggle between the Union and the republics concerns the distribution of expenditure and taxes. Although this issue has been very much politicized, it is useful to bring out the underlying economic considerations by applying arguments about fiscal federalism to the case of the Soviet Union.

The main insight from the literature on fiscal federalism is that the authority to tax should be delegated to the lowest possible level of government to match as closely as possible tax payments and tax benefits in the form of public goods produced. The constraint is found in the production technology of the public good (every township can have its own radio station and school, but not its own army). This general principle suggests that a large degree of fiscal decentralization would be appropriate for the Soviet Union, for, given its size and heterogeneity, there are large differences in the needs of the different republics. For example, a more developed republic might want to levy

31

higher taxes to finance the expenditure on social infrastructure (higher education, telecommunications, etc.) that is needed to sustain a modern industrial sector.

From a pure efficiency point of view, the power of the Union government to impose taxes (or to coordinate the actions of the republican governments) would thus be justified only by indivisibilities and external effects. This implies that the direct role of the Union government should be limited to defense, environment, infrastructure for long-distance transport, and so forth. It might also be necessary, however, to allow the Union government to coordinate republican fiscal policy in order to limit tax competition (by establishing a common value-added tax or a common principle of taxation of financial capital, for example).

This argument for a fundamental shift in fiscal authority from the Union to the republics might seem to be inconsistent with the dominant role of the central government in large Western countries. However, most of the powers the central governments have over taxes and expenditures have nothing to do with efficiency arguments; they are used to redistribute income. Income redistribution on such a large scale is motivated by the perception that all citizens of the country belong to one community that cares about its weaker members. This is certainly not true of the inhabitants of most of the republics of the Soviet Union. It would be appropriate, therefore, to limit the role of the Union government to those areas in which a central authority is necessary on efficiency grounds alone.

A Soviet Customs Union?

Despite the customs administrations instituted by some smaller republics, goods and services can still freely cross republican boundaries. The Soviet Union is thus still an *economic union*—a unified market within which goods, services, capital, and people can move without any obstacles. To obtain an idea of the level of the efficiency gains an integrated market can yield, it is useful to recall that the elimination of the remaining, small barriers to intra-EC trade by the Europe 1992 program is estimated to bring large economic benefits of up to 4 to 6 percent of the EC's GDP, according to the Commission of the European Communities (1988). If the Soviet Union were already a market economy, the trade barriers contemplated by some republics should thus imply very large economic costs indeed. There is, therefore, a strong *a priori* case against the imposition of customs borders between republics, which would break up the Soviet economic union. An exception to this general presumption is warranted, however, in two cases:

32

Temporary regional protection during the transition. Most theoretical arguments in favor of protection are based on the absence of a well-developed capital market that would allow producers to finance an initial period of learning by doing and the investment in capital and technology necessary to enable them to withstand international competition. Experience shows that it would take some time to create an efficient capital market in the republics, even in those that want to reform their economies as quickly as possible. Hence, there is a strictly economic rationale for republican protection during the transition. This applies, however, only to those goods for which prices are set administratively at lower levels in the rest of the Union. Temporary controls on the interrepublican movements of those goods might be justified to keep domestic producers from going bankrupt. Because very few goods are actually available on a large scale at their official prices, however, there are not likely to be many cases in which domestic producers need to be protected against "unfair" competition from the rest of the Union. On the contrary, it is more likely that other republics will impose bans on the exports of their own subsidized products. Accordingly, a republic that initiates reforms on its own will not need to impose customs barriers; if its reforms are successful, the rest of the Union will impose barriers for it.

Once a customs border is created, however, it produces a temptation to extend trade barriers to all trade, not just to the initially restricted goods. A fast transition toward a market economy would thus have the additional advantage that the disruption of internal trade by internal customs borders would be only temporary and limited to a small number of goods. Furthermore, a fast transition would minimize the temptation for individual republics to use overall protection to raise or preserve employment—a temptation that would be difficult to resist, for there will be considerable unemployment during a transition. The economic difficulties faced by Central Europe after World War I, with the disruption of established trade patterns by national protection, are a good example of the damage that could result if regional protection were to spread too far (for a detailed account of this period, see Kaser and Radice, 1985-86).

Is the Soviet Union an optimal customs union? A number of republics may want to establish their own commercial policies because any republic participating in the Soviet economic sphere would have to adopt the same barriers (tariffs or quotas) for world trade as the rest of the Soviet Union.[4] Once the transition period was over and regional protection had lost its justification, each republic would have to decide whether it would gain more from participating in world trade on its own or from participating in free trade within the Soviet Union but adopting the Union's trade barriers vis-à-vis the outside world.

The standard analysis of customs unions shows that the benefits from joining a customs union depend on several factors: (1) the degree of protection practiced by the union, (2) the size of the union, and (3) the size and economic structure of the participating economies.

In all likelihood, it will be some time before the Soviet Union adopts a liberal trade regime. This implies that the first factor—the degree of protection practiced—is already an argument for smaller republics to opt out and conduct their own commercial policies. Inside a Soviet customs union, they would import more high-cost products from the other republics and would thus lose as a result of the so-called trade-diversion effect.

The size of the union is relevant because, the larger the customs union, the more likely it is to contain the lowest-cost producers of most goods and therefore the less likely it is that trade diversion will take place. This aspect does not favor the Soviet Union, however, because it represents a market that is less than one-fifth the size of the European Community. Moreover, the Soviet Union will not be for some time the lowest-cost producer of the capital equipment most republics need to modernize their manufacturing industries. Remaining in the Soviet customs union would thus imply potentially large economic costs from trade diversion.

For these two reasons alone, the Soviet Union in its present form is not an attractive area for a customs union. But other considerations suggest even more strongly that some republics would definitely gain from leaving the Soviet customs union.

A by now widely accepted synthesis of the traditional comparative-advantage view and the modern view of trade based on economies of scale and product differentiation suggests that there will be intensive intraindustry trade between highly developed countries simultaneously with interindustry trade between countries with different capital-labor ratios (see Helpman and Krugman, 1985). There should be little trade,

---

[4] Another, more remote, possibility not discussed here is a mere free-trade area without any common external trade policy. A free-trade zone would represent the optimal solution from a theoretical point of view, but this is a policy any republic could pursue even in isolation by instituting unilateral free trade with all partners.

however, between countries with a similar capital-labor ratio that are not developed enough to specialize in the industrial goods exchanged within the group of rich countries.[5] Thus, trade between developed countries consists of the exchange of differentiated industrial goods produced with economies of scale but similar capital intensities, whereas the trade between rich countries with high capital-labor ratios and less-developed countries with low capital-labor ratios consists of an exchange of products with different capital-labor ratios.

This view of international trade can explain why numerous attempts to create customs unions in Latin America have all failed, suggesting that regional integration among less-developed economies is not very practical. Trade between the richer Latin American countries provides a particularly useful basis for comparison with the Soviet Union because their GDP per capita of $2,000 is close to estimates for the Soviet Union. A comparison of trade flows is shown in Table 2.

As shown in panel A of Table 2, Chile, with one of the highest GDP per capita ratios in Latin America, conducts only 20 percent of its trade within the region, but over 27 percent with the European Community and another 20 percent with the United States. The bilateral

TABLE 2

COUNTRY TRADE WITH ECONOMIC CENTERS, 1985–1988
(*percentage of average imports and exports*)

	Panel A			
	Brazil	Latin America	EC	United States
Argentina	11.0	26.7	28.7	15.5
Chile	7.6	20.5	27.5	20.7
	Panel B			
	Germany	USSR	EC	United States
Finland	13.5	16.4	41.8	5.5
Greece	21.6	2.3	60.2	5.3
Yugoslavia	12.9	19.9	33.3	5.7

SOURCE: International Monetary Fund, 1989.

[5] Balassa and Bauwens (1988) contain extensive tests of this view. Möbius and Schumacher (1990) provide a sectoral analysis of the trade of Eastern European countries that also confirms this general view.

trade flows between Argentina and Brazil are also interesting, because the relation between these two countries is similar to that between the Ukraine and Russia, at least in terms of population.[6] Only 11 percent of Argentina's foreign trade is with Brazil, but more than 28 percent is with the European Community. A customs union between Argentina and Brazil is therefore not likely to yield large economic benefits (unless the common external rate of protection is much lower than the present average of the two countries' national rates). On the contrary, such a customs union might actually be detrimental, because it might lead to more trade diversion than trade creation.

Among groups of countries at a similar level of development (for example, the OECD countries), the geographical distribution of trade flows is determined primarily by the so-called gravitational factors: distance, cultural affinity, and size of the different markets. Simple equations that embody these factors can account for about 80 percent of the cross-sectional variation in bilateral trade flows among European OECD countries.[7] These equations suggest that the overwhelming factor in determining the geographical distribution of trade flows is market size, which implies that the European Community is likely to become the dominant trade partner for all European countries and for the European Soviet republics.

The data in panel B of Table 2, on Finland, Greece, and Yugoslavia, confirm that trade with the European Community is very important, even for countries that are at its periphery. Indeed, even for a country like Finland, which is not a member of the European Community, Germany alone is almost as important a trading partner as is the Soviet Union (more recent data show that Finnish trade with the Soviet Union has fallen to about 10 percent of overall Finnish trade, reflecting in part the loss of politically motivated Finnish-Soviet trade in the past).

The Finnish example is particularly revealing because the Baltic Republics are in a similar position and of a similar size (Lithuania has about the same population as Finland). Our example suggests that the Baltic Republics would trade primarily with Western Europe if they were to become independent (and to be accorded the same trade preferences by the EC as Finland, a member of the EFTA). Hence, these republics have nothing to gain from participating in a Soviet customs union.

---

[6] The population of the Ukraine is 55 million (vs. 30 million for Argentina), and that of Russia is 140 million (the same as Brazil).

[7] See, for example, Aitken (1973). Balassa and Bauwens (1988) provide confirmation of the importance of gravitational factors on an industry-by-industry basis.

The Central Asian republics seem to represent a clear case in the other direction. They can be expected to trade intensively with the Soviet Union because of their lower level of development and their geographical position. Their gravitational attraction to the countries along the southern border (Iran, India), however, should not be underrated.

The Ukraine, Belorussia, and the Transcaucasian republics are in an intermediate position. The Ukraine and Belorussia have an industrial structure that suggests the possibility for intensive trade with Western Europe, but geography and cultural factors favor strong integration with Russia. In view of the Argentina-Brazil example cited above, however, the first effect might be stronger. Geography suggests that the Transcaucasian republics should trade intensively with the rest of the Soviet Union but also with the Middle East.[8]

We have argued so far that the trade patterns of established market economies suggest that a number of republics on the western edge of the Soviet Union might in the future trade much more with Western Europe than with each other. This argument is valid only if the trade links created in the past can be changed rather quickly. Krugman (1991) suggests, however, that historical accidents may have a permanent impact on trade. It is therefore interesting to consider the case of Yugoslavia, where the reform process started earlier. Yugoslav experience can be taken as an indicator of the speed with which the regional distribution of trade can change.

Between 1982 and 1988, Yugoslav exports to the CMEA countries (including the Soviet Union) declined from 44.8 to 26.3 percent of total exports, and imports declined from 29.8 to 21.0 percent. At the same time, Yugoslav exports to the European Community increased from 21.0 to 38.7 percent of total, and imports increased from 34.6 to 40.5 percent (International Monetary Fund, 1989). This rather substantial change in relative trade patterns (the EC and the CMEA essentially switched places) as a result of only partial reforms in Yugoslavia suggests that radical reforms might have a very large impact on the trade patterns of some republics in the five-year transition period considered necessary by the Union government for their smooth transition to independence.

The experience of Poland shows that the redirection of trade can at times be even more dramatic. In only one year, 1987, the share of industrial countries in Polish exports increased by over ten percentage

---

[8] See Commission, 1990c, annex 7, for an interesting application of a gravitational indicator to trade among Soviet republics and CMEA countries.

points (from 33 to 44 percent). This allowed the share of imports from that group of countries to increase by almost 15 percentage points (from 29 to 44 percent). The reform of 1990 continued this movement and led to a further increase in Polish exports to industrial countries by about 50 percent (Lipton and Sachs, 1990; Sachs, 1990).

Redirecting trade flows on this scale involves, of course, substantial adjustment costs, which might be lower if the adjustment were to move more slowly than in the case of Poland. But the data presented here suggest that trade with the West can very rapidly displace the established, planned trade flows and that their disruption is not apt to be as catastrophic as is often argued.

A Soviet Common Currency?

The introduction of a national currency would represent for some republics an important symbol of their independence. For certain republics, the introduction of a national currency can also be justified on purely economic grounds.

The literature on optimal-currency areas argues that the main advantage of having a national money is the ability to use the exchange rate to adjust to nationally differentiated shocks (Mundell, 1961). A more fundamental argument resides in the ability to choose a "monetary constitution," including a peg or anchor, to the most appropriate foreign currency. Different economic structures and social preferences yield different optimal choices. These advantages, however, have to be weighed against the gains from the ultimate degree of economic integration provided by a common currency.[9] This standard economic analysis of the costs and benefits of a monetary union can be applied to the case of the Soviet Union.

Introducing separate republican currencies would create a barrier to interrepublican trade by increasing transactions costs. The importance of this cost to splitting up the ruble area depends on the intensity of interrepublican trade and the efficiency of the payments and clearing system conducted in the ruble.

Estimates of interrepublican trade based on domestic prices are given in Table 3. It amounts to more than 30 percent of output for most of the smaller republics, including the three Baltic Republics, for which it amounts to about 50 percent. These republics should therefore be the

---

[9] For an evaluation of the economic costs and benefits of forming an economic and monetary union in the European Community, see Commission of the European Communities (1990b).

ones with the strongest interest in retaining the ruble. At present, however, the ruble does not provide any of the advantages of a common currency, for interrepublican trade is conducted by enterprises working through a complicated web of contracts involving republican and regional ministries (or other official bodies) and individual enterprises owned by the state (the Union, republic, or region), rather than through the market. The ruble thus does not fulfill the main function of money in trade among the republics. It is not the medium of exchange and thus cannot provide the benefits that otherwise arise from a common currency. This situation is not likely to change in the near future. Only in the long run, when all parts of the Soviet Union have become a market economy and are integrated in the world economy, can one expect the ruble to function effectively as a common currency.

Our judgment might seem to suggest that the smaller republics, which are already now very open to trade, should have at least a long-run interest in remaining in the ruble area. Yet, even a small republic that is not a viable currency area has an alternative to remaining in the ruble area. It can move closer to its preferred "monetary constitution" by

TABLE 3

TRADE DISTRIBUTION OF THE SOVIET REPUBLICS IN 1988
(*in percentage of GDP*) [a]

	Total	Domestic	Foreign	Population (millions)
Total USSR	30	21	8	284.5
RSFSR	22	13	9	146.5
Ukraine	34	27	7	51.4
Uzbekistan	40	34	5	19.6
Kazakhstan	34	29	4	16.5
Belorussia	52	45	7	10.1
Azerbaijan	41	35	5	6.9
Georgia	44	38	5	5.3
Tadzhikistan	44	38	6	5.0
Moldavia	52	46	6	4.2
Kirghizia	46	40	5	4.2
Lithuania	55	47	7	3.7
Armenia	54	48	5	3.5
Turkmenia	42	38	4	3.5
Latvia	54	47	7	2.7
Estonia	59	50	8	1.6

SOURCE: *Statistical Yearbook of the Soviet Union, 1990.*
[a] Assuming the same GDP/NMP ratio throughout the USSR.

joining another currency area. The attractiveness of this alternative depends on the geographical distribution of its trade. At present, all republics trade more with each other than with the outside world. For example, only about 15 to 20 percent of the total trade of the Baltic Republics is with the outside world. The opposite is true of a country like Finland, which is similar in geographical position population to Lithuania. Only about 11 percent of Finnish trade is with the Soviet Union, as opposed to over 40 percent with the European Community.

Once the Baltic Republics are integrated into the world economy, their trade patterns are likely to resemble those of Finland today, for reasons outlined above. In that case, they would gain more from joining the emerging European Monetary Union (EMU) than from remaining in the ruble area. This would not be true, however, as already noted, for the Central Asian and Transcaucasian republics, which are more likely to trade with the rest of the Soviet Union than with the European Community or other industrialized countries.

For the larger republics, mainly the Ukraine, interrepublican trade is less important relative to output (under 30 percent, comparable to the foreign-trade ratio of France, with approximately the same population). Hence, the economic argument for retaining the ruble is weaker. The larger republics are probably viable currency areas on their own. Moreover, as we argued above, a republic like the Ukraine might trade more with Western Europe than with Russia once the transition to a market system is completed. Even the Ukraine is unlikely to gain from keeping the ruble.

In summary, the main argument against national money at the republican level does not apply to the Soviet Union as long as the transformation to a market economy remains substantially incomplete. A fast reform process would increase interest in keeping the ruble on the part of those republics best prepared for a market economy. But, in the long run, only those republics that expect to trade more intensively with the rest of the Soviet Union than with the European Community should prefer the ruble to the European Currency Unit (ECU) as the alternative to their own republican currencies.

As noted above, the main advantage of a national currency is the ability to make exchange-rate changes when adjusting to nationally differentiated shocks. This advantage is particularly relevant for the Soviet Union, because the reform process will involve large regionally differentiated shocks.

The domestic aspects of the reform process are already a source of regionally differentiated shocks, because price reform will lead to large changes in relative prices and therefore to a significant redistribution of income, given the high degree of specialization of many republics and regions. Moreover, important aspects of the overall reform process may be determined and implemented by the individual republics (or even regions). Smaller republics with more developed administrative structures will therefore be able to reform their economies much faster than larger ones. This implies, in turn, that their real exchange rates vis-à-vis the rest of the Soviet Union may have to adjust considerably in the short run. This adjustment can be achieved through movements of domestic prices, but, given the size of the adjustment that may be required, substantial inflation or deflation may be the result. Freedom to change the nominal exchange rate can therefore be advantageous, particularly if it is difficult to reduce nominal wages. Those republics that would either lose from the freeing of prices or were slow to implement reforms would benefit most from being able to devalue vis-à-vis the rest of the Soviet Union. This would probably be the case for the Central Asian republics. For the Baltic Republics, the income loss from price reform (due principally to higher energy prices) might be offset by a faster reform process.

Once the initial shock of creating a market economy has been at least partly absorbed, the process of opening the Soviet Union to international trade will create another reason for changing exchange rates between republics. The republics that are close to major world markets for industrial goods and have diversified industrial structures supported by well-educated workers could expect to adapt more easily to international competition. This adjustment, however, would require a real appreciation vis-à-vis the less-developed republics. Retaining the ruble would therefore imply potentially large wage and price increases, which could be avoided if those republics had their own currencies and could alter the nominal exchange rates. Similarly, republics that would face a deterioration of their terms of trade could avoid deflationary pressures. This might be the case for some of the commodity-exporting republics of Central Asia. Three additional considerations reinforce the case for breaking up the Soviet monetary union.

Labor mobility is an important criterion used in the literature on optimal-currency areas, because a lack of wage flexibility can be offset by migration instead of by exchange-rate changes. But labor mobility in the Soviet Union will probably remain limited for some time because of the housing shortage, even though there are few legal obstacles to internal movement.[10] Moreover, in some republics, large-scale migration would be rejected on political grounds.

It is often argued that a monetary union should be supported by a fiscal framework that provides an implicit insurance mechanism, so that a region hit by an adverse shock would receive a transfer of income to compensate it at least partly for its inability to devalue its regional exchange rate. Such a mechanism is not likely to develop in a reformed Soviet Union, because the latest compromise reform plan says that most fiscal powers would remain in the hands of the republics, which would have to agree to any Unionwide unemployment insurance scheme.

Finally and most important, a common currency implies a common inflation rate in the long run. In the Soviet Union, inflation is already at the double-digit level, and a period of hyperinflation cannot be ruled out. Because all republics that retain the ruble will have to share in this inflation, those republics able to avoid the causes of hyperinflation—excessive fiscal deficits and wage indexation—have a strong incentive to introduce their own currencies.

---

[10] Residency permits for Moscow, which are accorded only in special cases, constitute one example of legal restrictions of internal labor mobility.

5   EXTERNAL CONSTRAINTS ON THE MEDIUM-TERM PROSPECTS OF THE SOVIET UNION

In this chapter, we shall assume that the Soviet Union manages to stay together, and we shall attempt to sharpen our understanding of Soviet growth prospects for the next decade or so. It is a necessary but hazardous attempt—necessary, because we need to know roughly where the Soviet Union is now to be able to project potential future growth; hazardous, because nobody has reliable data on the Soviet Union, not even the Soviets themselves. Different and changing methodologies, unreliable enterprise reporting, and, according to some Soviet experts, outright falsification make the task difficult. To illustrate, in March 1991, the new prime minister, Valentin Pavlov, stated that industrial production in January 1991 was down by 50 percent from January 1990; the Goskomstat (State Committee for Statistics) reported a decline of just 4 percent for the same period.

Discrepancies in data are not unique to the Soviet Union, but they are very pronounced there. We therefore compare estimates for the Soviet Union with those for Eastern Europe and for selected Western European countries and project growth scenarios in an effort to provide consistency checks. It is particularly important to know what the Soviet Union can achieve without Western assistance and to what extent rapid growth will depend on foreign investment. We conclude that even modest growth in the Soviet Union will require a large amount of foreign investment, which will be forthcoming only if a profound regime change occurs.

Because it is highly doubtful that the Soviet Union will be able to obtain foreign investments on a very substantial scale (more than $1,000 billion is needed for the next 10 to 15 years according to some estimates), priority must be given to foreign-exchange earnings. The reform of CMEA trade was an important step, but rapidly declining trade volumes have prevented the Soviet Union from benefiting fully. Attention needs to be concentrated on two key sectors: energy and agriculture. Energy accounted for nearly 40 percent of hard-currency exports in 1990, and agriculture for close to 20 percent of hard-currency imports. Both sectors have the potential for contributing much more positively to the trade balance, and we therefore devote one section to each sector. Many of the arguments developed for the energy sector also apply to other basic materials, in particular, to metals.[1]

The Soviet Union Compared to Eastern Europe

It is extremely difficult to assess the situation in Eastern Europe with any degree of precision, for there are no reliable data even for such basic macroeconomic variables as national income. Estimates for Soviet GDP in 1990 are close to R 950 billion. At the devalued commercial exchange rate of R 1.8 per dollar, this would equal $525 billion or $1,800 per capita. At the official exchange rate of R 0.6 in use before November 1990, GDP per capita would have been close to $5,400. In a country such as the Soviet Union, where prices bear no relation to social marginal cost and where exchange rates may move from drastic overvaluation to equally extreme undervaluation in very thin free markets, any currency conversion is problematic.

Table 4 collects some estimates of per capita income. Depending on the methodology employed, they vary on a scale from one to five. We

TABLE 4

ESTIMATED GDP PER CAPITA IN THE USSR AND EASTERN EUROPE IN 1990
(*in U.S. dollars*)

	(1)	(2)	(3)	(4)	Population (millions)
USSR	5,060	2,560	2,000	1,300	285.0
Czechoslovakia	7,940	2,680	1,985	1,700	15.6
Hungary	5,920	2,940	3,050	2,660	10.6
Poland	3,910	2,340	2,350	2,350	39.0

SOURCE: PlanEcon, 1990.
NOTE: Estimates in columns are based on:
(1) Purchasing-power parity, 1989-1990.
(2) Year-average commercial exchange rate, 1990.
(3) End-of-year commercial exchange rate, 1990.
(4) End-of-year free market rate, 1990.
Compare Portugal ($6,300), Greece ($6,600), and Spain ($12,400) at current prices and exchange rates (Commission, 1990d).

---

[1] The change in geopolitical conditions is also affecting sales of military equipment, an important traditional export item. This sector accounted for 25 percent of convertible-currency exports in 1988 and is expected to account for only 12 percent in 1991.

44

should therefore admit that we do not know how high current incomes are in the Soviet Union and Eastern Europe. What we regard as a "reasonable" estimate depends, of course, on the final use of the data. Estimates based on market exchange rates are reasonable assessments of potential import demand but are not reliable as a basis of comparison of income levels. The purchasing-power parity estimates in column (1) of Table 4 are more meaningful for this purpose. On this basis, Soviet income is about $5,000. We shall provide some evidence that this figure may be closer to the potential output of a reformed Soviet Union than the estimates in columns (2) and (3), which are preferred by most experts. Later, we shall use average incomes between $2,000 and $2,500 to remain close to the now dominant view, but we have serious doubts about the relevance of such estimates. There is, first, a problem of internal consistency. The estimate of Soviet income shown in column (2) is close to figures for Czechoslovakia and Hungary and underestimates the differences in living standards. It is also hard to believe that these Eastern European countries have average incomes that are less than half those of Portugal and Greece.

To show that an estimated current income close to $5,000 is quite reasonable, we add up the production of just three sectors valued at world market prices but omitting interindustry shipments, which are sizeable. We add only one more commodity to compensate for the omission (say, the production of steel, valued net of energy costs at $40 billion).

Soviet energy production, which accounted for about 11 percent of GDP in 1990 at current distorted prices, is worth close to $800 per capita at the world oil market price of $20 per barrel. Soviet agricultural production at world market prices, with a 100 percent markup for processing and distribution, is worth about the same. The military complex maintains an arsenal exceeding that of the United States, at least in quantitative terms, and U.S. defence expenditure accounts for over 5 percent of U.S. GDP, or more than $1,000 per capita. Hence, the world market value of these three sectors alone represents a potential productive capacity of $2,600 per capita. By implication, the commonly accepted estimate of $2,000 to $2,500 GDP per capita in the Soviet Union may not be overly pessimistic—unless, of course, there is no reform and no serious disarmament.

The inefficiency of resource allocation, especially in investment, is one of the explanations for low incomes in the Soviet Union and Eastern Europe. This becomes apparent in Table 5, which shows that Eastern European countries have been able to save a large share of GDP, with which they have financed high levels of investment. During the last five years, they have had no need to finance investment externally.

Yet, the very high shares of investment in GDP for the period 1985-89, ranging from 20 percent in Czechoslovakia to 30 percent in Poland and the Soviet Union, should have allowed potential output to grow at rates much higher than in Western Europe. The fact that output growth was significantly lower indicates that resource allocation and production incentives went astray. More positively, these figures suggest that rapid growth is possible in the future, even without foreign financial aid, if domestic resources can be used rationally and producers can be motivated. The essential requirement is internal reform and external finance.

To underline this point, Steinherr et al. (1990) compare incremental capital-output ratios (ICOR) over long time intervals and across regions. The ICOR is measured by the ratio of investment as a percentage of output to the annual average growth of output in real terms. The lower the ICOR, the more efficient investment is in generating more output. This analysis suggests that investment efficiency in the Soviet Union and in Eastern Europe deteriorated dramatically during the 1980s, just as it did in Africa. But, even during the 1970s, efficiency was comparable to that in Africa and fell significantly short of that in Asia. The ICORs of Table 5 confirm the deterioration during the 1980s. For the second half of the 1980s, ICORS reached their most inefficient levels, considerably higher than those of Portugal and Greece.

In terms of both purchasing-power parity income levels and savings capacity, Eastern Europe does not compare unfavorably with Portugal or Greece; social mismanagement is not the exclusive prerogative of Eastern European socialism. Yet, investment efficiency has been much

TABLE 5

GROWTH AND INVESTMENT IN THE USSR AND EASTERN EUROPE, 1985-1989
(*annual average percentages*)

	GDP Growth at Constant Prices	Growth of Gross Fixed Capital Formation at Constant Prices	Gross Fixed Capital Formation as percent of GDP	Savings as percent of GDP	Incremental Capital-Output Ratio
USSR	2.50	4.80	32.00	31.80	13
Czechoslovakia	1.65	2.40	19.87	23.40	12
Hungary	1.33	1.42	26.87	24.12	20
Poland	2.24	4.77	30.20	30.37	13
Portugal	4.24	10.74	23.80	17.10	6
Greece	2.02	1.92	18.60	n.a.	10

SOURCE: Institute of International Finance, 1990.

46

lower in Eastern Europe. As a consequence, foreign debt is a much more serious problem for Poland and Hungary, as the payment of interest alone would absorb between 5 and 7 percent of GDP.

Since January 1, 1991, trade within the CMEA has been priced and settled mainly in hard currencies. This is highly desirable for a more rational allocation of resources and therefore provides a net gain for the entire CMEA group. Nevertheless, some countries have lost out as the terms of trade have moved against them. In addition, net importers of energy will suffer if world oil prices increase. In both respects, the Soviet Union gains while other CMEA countries experience large terms-of-trade losses. The terms-of-trade gains to the Soviet Union amount to at least $6 billion, according to a recent study by the Commission of the European Communities (1990a).

Such computations also illustrate the exceptionally high vulnerability of the small Eastern European economies and of the Soviet Union to external shocks. The Soviet Union is a large country, but, if its GDP per capita in only $2,000, its total GDP is less than Italy's. Exports for hard currencies account for less than 10 percent of GDP, but the concentration of exportable goods (energy) makes for high terms-of-trade vulnerability.

External Financing Requirements for Various Growth Scenarios

Many regard the availability of foreign capital as the major constraint on growth in Eastern Europe. We shall therefore review the external financing requirements for rapid growth before considering more pessimistic scenarios. Our computations also provide useful insights concerning the probable speed of reconstruction and convergence with economic levels in the West.

The productivity gap between Eastern Europe and more advanced industrial countries can be attributed to three broad sets of factors. First, the economic system provides the wrong prices and little incentive for managers and workers to become more efficient. Second, the capital stock is insufficient and obsolete. And, third, the allocations of capital and manpower are distorted across sectors. Precise estimates are not possible, but it is generally considered that distortions in allocation and the lack of motivation, taken together, are as important as the inadequate capital stock. Thus, with an unchanged capital stock, reforms could potentially increase incomes enough to reduce the gap by half. We ignore this possibility in the scenarios below but shall demonstrate the potential for saving and for improved performance in external trade when we analyze the agricultural and energy sectors.

How much capital would be required to bring these Eastern European economies close to, say, the average income of the European Community? Because Eastern European countries aim at becoming members of the EC, this seems to be the most sensible basis for comparison and a useful benchmark. More realistically, and even taking into account the impatience widely felt about achieving a convergence of living standards, the countries of Eastern Europe will be doing well if they can achieve in the next ten years the average standard of living enjoyed by the EC countries in 1990.

In 1990, income per capita in the European Community was about $15,000 at constant 1988 prices, and it is expected to reach $20,000 by the year 2000. Table 6 takes as its starting point the estimates of Table 4 for income per capita in the Soviet Union and Eastern Europe, substantially scaled down from those in column (1) to reflect prevailing views.

The computations in Tables 7 and 8 are not forecasts but serve rather to check the resource costs of different growth paths over a time horizon of ten to fifteen years. In Table 6, a GDP per capita of $2,500 is used for the Soviet Union. If growth during the next ten years were to average 3 percent per year, income per capita by the year 2000 would be $3,350, or only slightly more than 20 percent of the present income of the European Community. To reach the EC's current income by the year 2000, the growth rate would need to increase to an

TABLE 6

CATCHING UP WITH WESTERN EUROPEAN STANDARDS OF 1990
(*in U.S. dollars, at 1988-90 prices and exchange rates*)

	(1) GDP per Capita in 1990	(2) GDP per Capita in 2000 at 3-percent Growth	(3) Required Rate of Growth to Catch Up by 2000	(4) Required Rate of Growth to Catch Up by 2005	(5) Net Capital Needs per Capita	(6) Savings at 20 percent of GDP per Capita (accumulated)
USSR	2,500	3,350	19.5%	12.5%	24,000	19,500 (15 years)
Czechoslovakia	6,000	8,060	9.5%	6.5%	15,600	16,200 (10 years)
Hungary	5,000	6,720	11.5%	7.5%	18,000	18,400 (12 years)
Poland	3,500	4,700	15.5%	10.5%	21,600	23,000 (15 years)

48

unattainable level of about 20 percent. Hence, impatience needs to be scaled down. Even over a horizon of fifteen years, the required rate of growth required would be 12.5 percent (column 4). Although not impossible in the light of East Asian experience, such a growth rate is very unlikely. Of course, by the year 2005, the per capita income in the European Community will be about $23,000 if growth averages 3 percent per year, so the Soviet Union's income would then amount to 60 percent of EC income, even though an "economic miracle" had occurred. The first lesson that emerges from Table 6, therefore, is that catching up will require more than one generation, even for the most advanced Eastern European countries. This lesson has considerable importance for the question of whether and when these countries can be integrated into the European Community.

Column 5 of Table 6 then computes the net capital needs (neglecting depreciation) for the growth paths of columns 3 and 4. This computation assumes an incremental capital-output ratio of 2, which corresponds to the average capital-output ratio for productive investment in the EC. It thus neglects depreciation, social investment, and the cost of an environmental cleanup but also neglects the potential efficiency gains from reforms through better use of existing resources. These may offset each other.

To accumulate the amounts of capital shown in column (5), a corresponding amount of domestic savings or foreign investment is required. Because some of the countries are already heavily indebted and foreign agents are still reluctant to invest, given the uncertainties, we need to know how much foreign capital is really required for the investment needs of column (5). Therefore, we must look at savings.

Domestic savings ratios for the period 1985-89 range from 24 percent in Czechoslovakia and Hungary to 30 percent in Poland and the Soviet Union,[2] but they are likely to fall from their forced levels in spite of

[2] There is frequent confusion about treatment of interest payments on the foreign debt and military expenditures in the national accounts. Strictly speaking, interest payments are costs and are not paid out of savings. As with any other expenditure, however, a fall in these costs would increase savings (*ceteris paribus*). Thus, high savings rates in the past were achieved in addition to servicing the foreign debt. For future scenarios, therefore, we do not subtract interest payments on the foreign debt. A similar argument pertains to military expenditures. They are a form of consumption and not a use of savings. If they are reduced, either consumption of other goods or investment can rise without changing savings. Particularly in the Soviet Union and Eastern Europe, we see a large scope for substituting welfare-generating consumption or investment for military expenditures.

possibly safer and higher returns. So far, these declines have not been dramatic, as the precautionary motive for saving plays a more significant role in a market economy. Increased uncertainty and insufficient state provisions for old age, sickness, and unemployment are bound to induce people to save.

Taking a conservative savings rate of 20 percent, Czechoslovakia could finance the investment required to catch up in ten years and could even achieve a slight surplus. Hungary would require twelve years, and Poland, fifteen years. The Soviet Union would need much more time, or foreign investment of more than $1,300 billion accumulated over fifteen years (the savings gap amounts to $4,500 per person).

These computations suggest that there is a fundamental difference between the Soviet Union and the other countries. Catching up with Western Europe's present income level over the next fifteen years is feasible for Czechoslovakia and Hungary, less so for Poland, but out of reach for the Soviet Union. Furthermore, the Soviet Union can get close to this level only if its present income is grossly underestimated and if foreign-capital contributions are significant. The size of the problem, however, may far exceed the capacity of the West, even if it is willing to support reform for political reasons.

These scenarios do not suggest that foreign capital will not be necessary for the Eastern European countries. They do suggest that even a scenario of high growth will not require much of an increase in foreign debt over the period as a whole. Foreign direct investment will be necessary to effect the transfer of technology and management skills and to assist in reallocating national resources.

Foreign funds will also be particularly useful during the initial years to finance the takeoff and to offset income losses generated by the shock of restructuring. This is very clearly evidenced by the Polish and Soviet experiences. Unfortunately, it is most difficult to borrow abroad at the beginning of a regime change, and it is therefore of utmost importance to establish credibility and creditworthiness as rapidly as possible. As long as foreign investors are not confident about a future return to stable growth with open borders, they will either not invest or invest only in projects with very short payback periods.

Table 7 repeats the exercise in Table 6 under three more pessimistic assumptions. First, we have scaled down income per capita at the starting point by as much as 30 percent. These estimates correspond, in our view, to plausible minima. Second, we assume an average growth rate of only 3 percent for the next decade. And, third, we assume that the entire existing capital stock needs to be depreciated during the decade. As a result of the first two assumptions, income levels in the year 2000 will fall short of today's average EC income level by more than 50 percent in Czechoslovakia and more than 80 percent in the Soviet Union. In comparison to expected EC income for the year 2000, Soviet income will fall short by 88 percent. We find it hard to believe, therefore, that such a scenario could be sustained. It would reflect the continuation of allocative inefficiencies and of disincentives that should give way under the pressure of economic misery. Under the third assumption, moreover, that the existing capital stock needs to be fully depreciated, domestic savings will be insufficient to finance even these dismal growth paths. The Soviet Union would require over $200 billion of net foreign capital over the next ten years just to increase its per capita income from $2,000 to $2,700.

All in all, our analysis suggests that there is a fundamental difference between the prospects of the Soviet Union and Eastern Europe. Starting income is lower in the former, and economic and political reforms still need to be carried out under much more conflicting conditions. Hence, an average Soviet growth rate of 5 percent for the next decade is already quite optimistic. We do not believe, therefore, that the Soviet Union can reach even one-third of current EC income by the year 2000.

The pessimistic scenarios in Table 7 represent, in fact, a catastrophe. The 3-percent growth scenario for the Soviet Union would require a foreign contribution of $230 billion. Changing the growth assumption to 5 percent would increase this amount to $390 billion, and adding on the accumulated interest plus the already existing debt of about $60 billion would bring the external debt to over $700 billion by the year 2000. Because the West would be unlikely to provide credits and

TABLE 7

EXTERNAL CONSTRAINTS UNDER MORE PESSIMISTIC ASSUMPTIONS
(in U.S. dollars, at 1988-90 prices and exchange rates)

	(1) GDP per Capita in 1990	(2) GDP per Capita in 2000 at 3-percent Growth	(3) Gross Capital Needs per Capita	(4) Savings at 20% of GDP Accumulated to 2000	(5) Accumulated Trade- Account Deficit per Capita	(6) Accumulated Trade- Account Deficit (billions)
USSR	2,000	2,700	5,400	4,600	800	228
Czechoslovakia	5,000	6,700	13,400	11,400	2,000	31
Hungary	3,500	4,700	9,400	8,000	1,400	15
Poland	2,500	3,400	6,800	5,700	1,100	43

financial aid so generously, even such a pessimistic scenario may be infeasible, and all the weight of a slow and painful adjustment would be thrown onto Soviet citizens. We cannot believe they would accept prospects of this sort, and we would expect, instead, a strong pressure for exiting, either individually through emigration or collectively through secession in line with the analysis in Chapter 4.[3]

As our previous discussion made clear, there is a high probability that the starting point of our growth scenarios, a GDP per capita between $2,000 and $2,500, is a serious underestimate. We may also have underestimated the capacity of the Soviet system to respond to generous Western support (conditional on widespread reforms) and overestimated the power of the traditional, reform-adverse institutions. All this would be necessary to justify a "grand bargain" trading reform for aid, as proposed by some Western and Soviet experts (*Financial Times*, May 22, 1991). The same experts propose a financial package of $15 to $30 billion a year for about ten years. Our scenarios suggest that this will be too little to bring about a drastic turnaround, assuring successful political pluralization and coherent market reforms—it may merely serve to keep the system stumbling along.

Agriculture

In all Eastern European countries, the effects of collective ownership and centralized planning have been most disastrous in agriculture, but the worst situation is to be found in the Soviet Union. This is best illustrated by the fact that the Soviet Union is a net importer of agricultural products, although its arable land surface is far larger than China's, which feeds more than one billion people. What are the prospects for Soviet agriculture? We concentrate on the potential rather than the expected scenario.

Collectivization of agriculture in the Soviet Union began in the 1930s, about twenty years earlier than in Eastern Europe. The destruction of the traditional peasantry is therefore more complete. In addition, collective farms are larger and more dominant in Soviet agriculture, so

---

[3] Throughout this chapter, we have implicitly assumed that the labor force in Eastern Europe remains constant. Demographic trends suggest that this assumption is correct. Participation rates are already higher than in Western Europe, so further increases are unlikely. With open borders, however, large income differentials between East and West would provide a strong incentive to westward migration, particularly if growth in Eastern Europe proceeds slowly. Such migration would become a pronounced phenomenon, accelerating factor-price (income) equalization between East and West.

that the division of labor is more pronounced. Low pay and long distances to urban centers have made living conditions in the countryside so dismal that people with the slightest skills have left for urban centers. Hence, one major obstacle to reconstructing Soviet agriculture will be the low skill level of the rural population. For this reason, if no other, any comparison to Chinese reforms is misleading. Chinese farmers are highly skilled and have demonstrated their ability to respond strongly to price incentives. Soviet farming is, of course, less labor intensive than Chinese farming, and the relative importance of equipment and fertilizers is correspondingly greater, but what seems to be most lacking is management. Western assistance in managing and equipping production, distribution, and processing might make a very important contribution.

Three, not mutually exclusive, arguments are advanced to explain the low efficiency and the resulting import dependency of Soviet agriculture. One points to the harsh climate and low soil fertility that make production more intensive in the use of manpower, energy, and fertilizers and more dependent on weather conditions. A second cites the model of socialist planning, which not only emphasized the development of heavy industry to the neglect of agriculture but also organized agriculture on the industrial model, destroying the traditional peasantry (the kulaks) and creating large collective farms run by socialist managers and specialized agricultural workers. This second argument points to the low productivity resulting from inefficient organization and the lack of individual motivation, and also to the inefficiencies of transport, storage, distribution, and transformation that cause abnormally high losses. A third argument cites the pricing system, which provides inadequate producer incentives. We discuss these issues in turn.

Climatic and weather conditions. The Soviet Union's arable land, permanent pastures, and forests substantially exceed those of any other large nation (see Table 8). However, soil quality and climatic conditions account for exceptionally high variations in land productivity.

Crop farming is concentrated in the grain belt, covering one-eighth of the Soviet territory and extending from the northwest southeastward into Kazakhstan and Western Siberia. The two principal environmental problems are high latitude with long winters and extreme continentality accounting for increasing moisture loss toward the south and east. Only in the Baltic Republics and Belorussia can the annual precipitation reach 1,000 millimeters; most of the grain belt receives only 200 to 600 millimeters.

Southeast of the Baltic coast is the famous *chernozem* (black soil) belt,

53

with fertile top soil and the best combination of moisture and heat resources. It stretches from Belorussia through the Ukraine down to the Black Sea. To the southeast are the southern plains, with generous heat conditions but declining moisture. These steppe soils, like the black soils, are well drained and cultivable.

The differences in environmental conditions are of obvious economic importance. In particular, output is somewhat weather-dependent and therefore variable in each subregion. According to results obtained by Desai (1987), however, weather conditions in the western and eastern parts of the grain belt are relatively constant and do not greatly affect the differences in total annual grain yields. As a consequence, the variability of aggregate output caused by weather conditions is smaller than often assumed. The standard deviation of yield variability was 12.3 percent of the mean yield from 1955 to 1982 (Desai, 1987, pp. 218-220;

TABLE 8

SOVIET AGRICULTURE IN INTERNATIONAL COMPARISON

	USSR	China	U.S.	Western Europe
Land Area in 1988 (1,000 ha)	2,227,200	932,691	916,660	372,487
Arable	227,700	93,345	187,881	82,422
Permanent crops	4,726	3,300	2,034	12,018
Permanent pasture	371,800	319,080	241,467	68,354
Forest and woodland	945,000	117,115	265,188	128,236
Irrigation (1,000 ha)				
1973	12,746	40,852	16,510	8,861
1988	20,782	44,938	18,102	11,501
Tractors in use in 1988 (1,000)	2,692	876	4,670	8,573
Percentage of population in agriculture				
1980	20.0%	74.2%	3.5%	10.4%
1989	13.6%	68.2%	2.4%	7.1%
Production in 1989 (1979-1981 = 100)				
Livestock	125.1	188.6	109.8	106.0
Cereals	127.8	129.3	93.3	117.9
Yield (kg/ha)				
Cereals	1,905	4,014	4,410	4,503
Potatoes	11,613	11,550	32,160	25,100
Cotton	2,529	2,193	1,819	2,727

SOURCE: Food and Agriculture Organization of the United Nations, 1989.

in some years, however, weather variability was up to 22 percent of average yield). Only 52 percent of this variance in agricultural yield is explained by weather fluctuations; the remainder is explained by input variations. Hence, the importance of weather conditions should not be exaggerated.

The results are not very different from those obtained in North America, where climate and soil variations are comparatively large (Desai, 1987). What is fundamentally different is the influence of production organization and of price effects. In years of above-average crops in the Soviet Union, inflexibility in the use of manpower and machinery creates large discrepancies between potential and harvested crops. This limits variability. However, the lack of price flexibility increases variability, because prices do not increase in bad years to induce greater production efforts. Moreover, procurement prices vary inversely with productivity, increasing the share of low-productivity areas, where output is also more volatile.

Socialist planning and organization of production. Since private ownership of land was abolished in the winter of 1917-18, land has been used by state farms, collective farms, other state organizations, and private individuals. Those who defend the status quo emphasize the ability of collective and state farms to finance and construct infra-structure and to wield their bargaining power with the supply organization. They also point out that the great majority of farmers do not want changes in property rights for fear of losing social protection. A radical dissenting view, expressed by Boris Yeltsin, is that "the land should be given back to the peasants. How it should be farmed, whether by collective farms, state farms, small private farms, or single individuals, should be decided by the peasants themselves, and nobody else" (Second USSR Congress of People's Deputies, December 1989).

Table 8 allows a comparison of Soviet productivity with China, the United States, and Western Europe. With some exceptions (cotton, for example), the Soviet levels are low by international standards. This low productivity can be traced to a comparative lack of skills and motivation of Soviet agricultural workers, to inadequate allocation of resources, and to a great variability in available and usable machinery and inputs.

Inadequacies in resource allocation have not been caused primarily from inadequate funding. During 1975-86, agriculture and the agro-industrial sector received investment funds amounting to about one-third of all investment allocated through the state budget, with about 80 percent of that allocation channelled into agriculture and the remainder to related industries. One might argue that productivity problems have

55

been mainly related to the structure rather than to the level of capital investments. Insufficient attention has been given to the allocation, maintenance, and efficient use of capital equipment. Too much investment has gone into large-scale construction and land-reclamation projects and too little into reliable equipment, retooling, and maintenance.[4]

As argued by the U.S. Department of Agriculture (1990), the inadequate quantity and quality of variable inputs (seeds, fertilizers, and feedstuffs) and slowness in adopting modern agronomic methods have limited the productivity of capital. Input deficiencies in some areas cut the productivity of all other inputs. From 1970 to 1987, use of fertilizers increased by 270 percent and use of pesticides by 240 percent, but the use of tractors and trucks increased by less than 20 percent, and agricultural output rose only 20 percent. During the same period, the output-capital ratio fell by about 40 percent.[5] Mechanized agriculture requires developing suitable crop varieties, but less than 10 percent of vegetable cultures have even partly met requirements for mechanical harvesting and processing. Inadequate use of fertilizers and, in some areas, excessive irrigation have significantly impaired soil quality even in the most fertile regions. The main cause for low output is lack of decentralization to adapt the use of fertilizers, pesticides, and irrigation to the specific local needs.

Problems in processing food are commensurable with those in producing it. From 1975 to 1987, fixed productive capital in the sector rose by 90 percent, yet output rose by only 40 percent. Less than 20 percent of the vegetable crop and only 2 percent of the potato crop are processed, despite the need for processing in a country where storage and distribution facilities are grossly underdeveloped. Annual potato and vegetable production is about 100 million tons, yet storage capacity

---

[4] Projects also suffer from excessive completion time, so that obsolescence is built in from the start. In the case of sugar refineries, where capacity is grossly inadequate, only 10 percent of the R 385 million allocated to major repairs and new construction from 1986 to 1990 was spent by the end of 1989 (U.S. Department of Agriculture, 1990, p. 48).

[5] Even more devastating than these measures based on output are the results in terms of value added. The Soviet machine-building industry allocates more than 30 percent of its total output to the agricultural complex; the energy-producing industry, 28 percent; the metallurgy and chemical industry, 32 percent; and the construction industry, 35 percent. Nevertheless, 70 percent of all agricultural operations are still performed manually (U.S. Department of Agriculture, 1990). By comparison, in OECD countries, supplies to the agricultural and food sectors represent, at most, 7 percent of output (that of the chemical industry). Soviet definitions, however, are more extensive and include transport and distribution.

is only 22 million tons. Joint ventures with Western firms could prove particularly efficient in this sector.

Pricing and budgetary implications. Agriculture has been singled out in the government programs for 1990 and 1991 for increased investment funding, even though investment is declining throughout the economy. The basic strategy is still, however, to rely on centralized decisionmaking and increased resource flows, with little attention given to incentives for improving quality or for the efficient use of resources. Policy focuses on shifting the supply curve and totally ignores movement along it.

The logic of the 1982 food program—still largely maintained—is to provide inefficient state and collective farms with the resources necessary to survive. The main policy tools have been highly differentiated procurement prices and lax credit policies (negative real interest rates, premiums for financial distress added to procurement prices, debt write-offs, etc.). This policy has had far-reaching consequences.

First, it has not helped to increase efficiency. Because procurement prices are low for efficient producers and high for less efficient producers, producer surplus is expropriated from efficient producers. Why this should be necessary in a socialist economy is not entirely clear, but it discourages an expansion of production by efficient producers. For example, the low-cost wheat-producing areas, where much of the best wheat is grown, receive the lowest state procurement prices. At the same time, the price that the state charges for mixed feeds is uniform throughout the country and can be twice as high as the price of wheat in the low-cost regions. Hence, farms in these regions have a strong incentive to feed their high-quality wheat to their livestock.

Second, the average level of agricultural-produce prices relative to the average level of industrial-goods prices has fallen steadily since 1975. This explains the difficult financial situation of most collective farms and the dilapidated state of the capital stock.

Third, retail prices of many basic food products, notably livestock products such as meat and milk, are below state procurement prices (for meat, sometimes less than one-third; see Ellman, 1991). This price difference is covered by state subsidies. In the 1990 budget, food subsidies amounted to R 95 billion or 20 percent of total budget expenditure, 10 percent of GDP, and 160 percent of the budget deficit. Moreover, these subsidies mostly benefit higher-income groups (meat is not affordable for lower-income groups and is less available outside large cities).

There are other budget expenditures on agriculture (investment, operational expenses). All in all, these accounted for 12 percent of

GDP in 1990. It seems, therefore, of utmost importance to reduce subsidies, eliminate differentiated producer prices, and introduce some price flexibility in response to supply in order to control the budget, reduce the trade deficit, and increase consumer satisfaction. Furthermore, in view of the inefficiency and very high spoilage rates of the present marketing system, it would be sensible to allow private traders to enter the market. This would require legal adaptations, however, for "speculation" (buying and selling a product at different prices) is a criminal offence under Soviet law.

Foreign-trade implications. In our view, the Soviet Union should be able gradually to reduce agricultural imports and to become a net exporter. Price liberalization, private ownership, and foreign assistance would be enough to ensure this.[6] Whether these reforms will come about soon, however, is highly debatable.

We see the long-run Soviet opportunities in the excellent quality of the soil in the southeastern and eastern Soviet Union, combined with the proximity of the European Community, the largest market in the world. Northern, Central, and Southern Europe are all accessible through waterways, assuring transport costs competitive with trans-Atlantic costs. The vital question is whether the EC market for agricultural products will be opened up. We see some grounds for guarded optimism.

It will become very awkward for the European Community to keep its agricultural markets closed to imports from the Soviet Union and Eastern Europe, for the most effective help Europe can give is to open its markets, including its agricultural markets. Maintaining the Common Agricultural Policy (CAP) in its present form will be increasingly difficult because of the high resource cost, the political conflicts created by the dumping of European surpluses, and the environmental problems caused by overproduction.

When agriculture in the Soviet Union and Eastern Europe produces at a "normal" level, the effect on world prices, and hence on the CAP, will be dramatic. Therefore, Europe can make an important and self-interested contribution by reducing its own production to or below its own level of consumption and thus providing scope for Eastern European production without steep price cuts on world markets.

With the CAP relaxed, imports from Eastern Europe can substitute

[6] Our long-term analyses yield much more optimistic scenarios than the short-term arguments in Begg et al. (1990). Their study expects, however, an increase in Soviet wheat production of at least 30 percent, representing 5 percent of present world production.

for EC production. In the longer run, it is perfectly reasonable to go even a step further. Animal husbandry in the EC uses high-cost domestic or cheap imported feedstuffs and causes serious environmental problems in the most efficient, and hence dense, production centers. Europe's environment is a very expensive production factor, and its cost rises much faster than in the vast spaces of the Soviet Union and Eastern Europe. It would therefore be desirable to reduce animal husbandry in the EC and to transfer production to the East. Instead of exporting animal feedstuffs, the Soviet Union and Eastern Europe would then have the opportunity to export products with high value added (meat and dairy products, for example).

We therefore conclude this section optimistically. Soviet agriculture has export capacity in the long run if it manages to introduce private property, to reform prices, and to secure Western support for improving food storage, processing, and distribution. In addition, it needs access to European markets, and this should not prove impossible over the long term. Providing these markets is arguably the greatest contribution Western Europe can make to Soviet and Eastern European development.

Energy

After agriculture and the military complex, energy is the most important sector of the Soviet economy. According to official sources, its output accounts for 10.8 percent of total output. At world market prices, the value of output in 1990 was equal to $240 billion, so the share of energy was at least 15 percent of GDP at $5,000 per capita and over 30 percent for lower GDP estimates.

Energy is even more important in the Soviet Union's foreign trade, accounting for 50 percent of hard-currency earnings. The Soviet Union is the largest producer of energy (and oil) in the world and, after Saudi Arabia, the largest oil exporter.

Given the very great need for imports of equipment and consumer goods, the only slowly rising export potential of agriculture, and the difficulty of substantially increasing foreign debt, energy exports will remain essential. We have already noted that hard-currency pricing of energy exports to CMEA countries is producing substantial terms-of-trade gains. In recent years, about 50 percent of energy exports went to socialist countries at below world market prices. Evaluated at $20 per barrel, these exports could have generated receipts of $40 billion, or more than the total Soviet hard-currency exports in 1990. In fact, however, petroleum exports generated hard-currency revenues not much greater than $12 billion.

Of central importance, therefore, is whether income from energy can be sustained or even increased over the years to come. Pessimism is widespread for several reasons. Some of the most easily accessible oil fields are now depleted, and the cost of exploitation is rising. According to official sources, the cost of oil extraction has tripled since 1985.

Table 9 shows that oil production has actually decreased since 1980. This decrease was more than offset by the increase in natural-gas production (the Soviet Union is estimated to hold 40 percent of world reserves), but domestic consumption rose in line with supplies. Production, transport, and refining facilities are inefficient and grossly wasteful. Soviet oil refineries are technologically backward and lack hydrocracking and catalytic units. As a consequence, the share of heavy oils, which must be sold at unattractive prices, remains excessive. Finally, security aspects have stopped expansion of nuclear energy production and caused stoppages of gas transportation and resistance to further development. In June 1989, the explosion of the Siberia-Volga gas pipeline at Ufa caused the death of about 1,000 people and demonstrated that the lack of technological control was not confined to nuclear power stations. About one-third of the existing gas pipelines have polymeric insulation, reliable for ten years, but planned to be in use for thirty.

Energy waste in domestic consumption remains at record levels. The ratio of energy use to GDP is about four times that of Western Europe and twice that of the United States.[7] Reducing this waste will require, first of all, moving energy prices *gradually* to world market levels, for the installation of meters for private consumption and the reequipping of industry will be costly and will require time. Furthermore, a rapid increase in prices would render much existing equipment obsolete. Prices could be raised across a five-year period, after a substantial initial increase. In the interim, tax penalties could be used to increase the energy efficiency of new equipment.

A reduction of the energy to GDP ratio by 3 percent per year over the next ten to twenty years seems quite feasible in light of recent OECD experience. Between 1972 and 1989, the energy intensity of real GDP in the United States fell by 28 percent; in the European Community, it fell by 20 percent. The oil intensity of output has fallen by about 35 percent and 40 percent, respectively (*Economic Report of*

---

[7] According to estimates by the International Energy Agency (1990), the Soviet Union used 1 toe per $1,000 of GDP in 1988, as compared to 0.4 toe for OECD countries. The ratio of 2.5 is lower than our estimate of 4 because the Agency used a much higher GDP estimate.

the President, 1991; Commission of the European Communities, 1990d). These reductions were achieved in spite of the ultimately negligible energy-price increases in real terms for final energy users. Between 1972 and 1989, energy prices in the U.S. consumer price index increased by only 17 percent over nonenergy items. Therefore, in the Soviet Union, a quite substantial increase in energy prices relative to nonenergy prices, combined with a restructuring of industry (which has also contributed to energy savings in the OECD countries, but in smaller proportions), should be able to achieve comparable reductions in energy intensities.

Table 9 sets out different forecasts for Soviet energy production, consumption, and exports. A peak for total energy production was reached in 1988-89. By the year 2000, oil production will have declined

TABLE 9

ENERGY EXPORT POTENTIAL OF THE USSR

(*in million tons oil equivalent*)

	1980	1990	2000	
			(1) [a]	(2) [b]
Total energy production [c]	1,380	1,680	1,300	1,630
Oil	605	580	480	540
Gas	360	660	785	890
Total energy consumption	1,160	1,410	1,000	1,300
Oil	450	420	n.a.	n.a.
Gas	320	580	n.a.	n.a.
Total net exports	215	265		
Oil	155	160 }	300-630	0-330
Gas	40	80 }		
Earnings (billions)		$40 [d]	$36-80	$0-40
Ratio of energy to GDP (multiple of Western Europe)		4	3	4

[a] Estimates for production from Korchemkin, 1990; for consumption, export, and energy-to-GDP ratios from authors' computations assuming GDP annual growth at 3%, annual gain on energy efficiency at 3%, and domestic use of oil and gas only.

[b] Estimates for production from Sagers, 1990; for consumption, export, and energy-to-GDP ratios from authors' computations assuming GDP annual growth at 3%, unchanged energy efficiency, and domestic use of gas and oil only.

[c] Includes coal and hydropower.

[d] At $20/barrel.

further, natural-gas production will have increased, but overall energy production will actually be lower than in 1990.

Resources for investment in the energy sector are declining and will remain insufficient during the years to come. During the 1980s, the energy sector absorbed about 20 percent of overall investment, with a net acceleration between 1985 (14 percent) and 1988 (24 percent).[8] The heavy emphasis on energy investments represented a drag on resources available for investments elsewhere and mainly served to maintain wasteful energy consumption. In addition, the productivity of new investments has been doubtful. According to several reports, even physical productivity is sometimes negative (that is, it sometimes requires more than one unit of energy to increase supply to users by one unit). This huge absorption of resources without corresponding returns contributed significantly to the overall economic downturn. It will be essential in the future to reduce costs by using energy more efficiently rather than by simply increasing production. In the energy sector itself, investment should be focused on more efficient technology in production, transport, and refining, not on expanding extraction. The largest investment, however, will be required on the user side; existing equipment must be replaced by more energy-efficient machinery.

Table 10 gives information on sectoral energy intensities. It shows that the inefficient use of energy is much higher in certain sectors than is suggested by overall data and suggests that reforms could start most fruitfully in these sectors. Because these sectors represent a disproportionate share of overall economic activity (larger than in the West), the savings would be particularly large (by contrast, the least energy-intensive sector, services, accounts for only 27 percent of Soviet GDP, as compared to over 50 percent in the OECD countries).

The Energy Research Institute of the Soviet Academy of Science estimates that use of appropriate technology could save up to 520 million tons oil equivalent (mtoe), or more than one-third of use in 1990. This would take some time, but a reduction of energy intensity at a rate of 3 percent per year appears to be feasible. The International Energy Agency (1990) estimates potential savings by using Canadian standards (technology and economic structure) and arrives at 463 mtoe, of which 264 mtoe savings would be efficiency gains and 199 mtoe structural gains.

---

[8] The structure of energy production changed markedly between 1980 and 1990. The share of natural gas increased from 26 to 38 percent, oil declined from 44 to 36 percent, coal declined from 23 to 18 percent, and primary energy increased from 4 to 6 percent.

Future consumption depends on the growth of the Soviet economy and the efficiency of energy use. For consistency with previous scenarios, we assume an average growth rate of 3 percent per year up to the year 2000. Returning to Table 9, we employ two assumptions with regard to energy efficiency. The pessimistic assumption is based on an unchanged energy to GDP ratio, equal to four times that of Western Europe. This appears overly pessimistic to us, as it would not allow any room for price and structural reforms. We therefore present a scenario for an efficiency gain from a level of four to a level of three, or 3 percent annually, which appears modest in light of the exorbitant waste that currently takes place. As inefficiencies vary substantially across activities, structural reforms (for example, the scaling down of heavy industries, which are among the most inefficient energy users) will significantly increase energy efficiency gains.

On these assumptions, the range for the export potential stretches from zero to $80 billion in 2000, at an assumed price of $20 per barrel. The lower bound would be catastrophic but, happily, is unlikely; it

TABLE 10

ENERGY INTENSITIES IN THE USSR, CANADA, AND EUROPE, 1980 AND 1988

(*in toe per thousand U.S. dollars of output*)

	USSR		Canada		Europe	
	1980	1988	1980	1988	1980	1988
Production sector						
Industry	1.50	1.55	1.38	1.25	0.59	0.54
Energy [a]	2.16	2.55	2.43	2.38	2.22	2.21
Basic industry	2.10	2.09	1.78	1.48	0.85	0.64
Refining & chemicals	1.91	1.68	1.73	1.37	0.62	0.42
Nonmetallic minerals	1.68	1.66	0.89	0.84	0.72	0.78
Basic metals	2.43	2.65	2.16	1.94	1.53	1.22
Other industry	0.71	0.59	0.60	0.45	0.18	0.14
Construction	0.22	0.15	0.06	0.04	0.02	0.02
Agriculture	0.29	0.34	0.20	0.23	0.14	0.16
Commercial transport	1.29	1.17	1.91	1.48	n.a.	n.a
Services [b]	0.15	0.13	0.11	0.09	0.07	0.05
(*in kg of oil equivalent per square meter*)						
Residential Sector	36.8	32.1	27.5	22.6	18.5	17.5

SOURCE: International Energy Agency, 1990.

NOTE: Europe is represented by France, Germany, Italy, and the United Kingdom.

[a] Includes nonenergy mining and water utilities but excludes refineries.

[b] Includes communications but excludes commercial transportation.

would occur only in the absence of any efficiency improvement and with a production level at about 20 percent below that of 1990. The higher bound of $80 billion is based on a reasonable efficiency gain and a higher production level (but still slightly below the 1990 level).

Because reasonably rapid development and reconstruction of the Soviet Union (at a 3-percent growth rate per year) will not be feasible without a substantial contribution from the energy and agricultural sectors, several important lessons emerge from Table 9.

First, major efforts must be made on both the production and consumption sides in order to generate a large surplus for energy exports. Given the technology and capital requirements, Western resources will be needed. Their provision, however, should be conditional on price and structural reforms.

Second, given the exorbitant waste of energy, a rapid price reform is mandatory. The effects on industry and consumers could be spread over several years, but all new equipment should be obliged to be energy efficient. If such a policy were carried out consistently, our 25-percent gain in energy efficiency would be attainable. In our discussion on growth scenarios, we experimented with the extreme assumption of replacing the entire capital stock over a ten-year period. Although this might be excessive, a 50-percent replacement would seem quite normal. With a growth rate of 3 percent per year, about two-thirds of the 1990 capital stock would be replaced by the year 2000 and thus be energy efficient. The efficiency level could double, and annual net exports could rise to as much as $120 billion.

Third, under any scenario, oil will play a reduced role and natural gas an expanded one. Will export markets exist for this natural gas? Western European supplies are more readily available (Netherlands, Norway, Algeria) for natural gas than for oil, and any shift to Soviet gas would require political negotiations and a redesigning of transport networks. Inspired by these requirements and the need for massive Western assistance to the Soviet energy sector, the Dutch prime minister, Ruud Lubbers, has proposed a European Energy Charter (EECH; Ludlow and Ross, 1990).

Lubbers' proposal is an example of policy proposals taking their inspiration from Western European integration; the EECH as a sectoral approach is inspired by the experience of the European Coal and Steel Community (ECSC). Similarly, plans for an Eastern European Payments Union (EEPU) are inspired by the European Payments Union (EPU), and the creation of the European Bank for Reconstruction and Development (EBRD) parallels the role of the European Investment Bank (EIB).

Steinherr et al. (1990) argue, however, that the EPU experience is not relevant under present conditions. Is this also the case for the EECH? Let us first survey the arguments in favor.

The ECSC was created for both political and economic reasons. The political aim was to control Germany's iron and steel industry and thereby control the key sector for economic growth and the defence industry. Economically, the idea was to manage politically a market where economies of scale in production had given rise to production cartels. Similar motivations underlie the EECH proposal. With energy as the key industrial sector, opening up to Western influence would enormously facilitate the restructuring of the Soviet economy. At the very least, Western investments in the Soviet energy sector could be facilitated by reducing sovereign and industrial risks within an integrated framework. Because energy efficiency depends on reforms embracing the whole economy (price and structural reforms), the conditions attached to Western intervention could have an economywide effect. The magnitude of the energy problem and its key role suggest the energy sector as an efficient level for reforms.

It would also be possible to negotiate long-term contracts and the development of a transport network spanning the European continent. Given the externalities and economies of scale, a planned approach of this kind might be economically justifiable. This could also apply to a common management of environmental problems. The Chernobyl disaster has demonstrated that the externalities involved can affect the entire continent. Reduced nuclear-energy production in the Soviet Union might thus be financially compensated within such a framework. These are the considerations that weigh in favor of an EECH. But there are also considerable difficulties.

First, it is not yet clear with which Soviet partner such a scheme should be negotiated, the Union or the republics. Once this question has been settled, it will most likely involve the Union and several republics. It is by no means evident that they will all accept loss of sovereignty over such a key sector.

Second, the European scale of the project is necessary but hardly sufficient. Most of the energy resources are located in Siberia and could also be exported to Asia. Moreover, U.S. oil companies have already started to invest in the Soviet Union, and one would hope that they will be massively involved. Thirty-five countries and international organizations participated in the first organizational meeting in Brussels in July 1991, so that participation by non-European partners seems assured.

Finally, the approach would need to respect meticulously the priority

65

for market solutions, that is, to deal only with those problems that the private sector cannot solve. The ECSC was a supranational authority with a heavy *dirigiste* orientation. This would not be feasible or desirable in the case of an EECH, which should support market-oriented solutions.

6 CONCLUSION

We have attempted in this study to describe the problems that can arise in the transition to a market economy and the ways they might be solved under the specific circumstances of the Soviet Union. Our main findings are as follows:

Because a market economy is one indivisible entity, partial reforms are doomed to failure, as experience has repeatedly shown. In addition, a lengthy reform process is likely to make matters initially even worse and to jeopardize the entire reform program. A comprehensive and coherent reform package that is implemented at once (to the extent this is possible) is therefore the best solution.

The elements of such a package are well known and include (1) price and wage liberalization, (2) financial reform and the creation of a two-tier banking system, (3) fiscal reform, and (4) privatization. The first two elements can be implemented rapidly—within less than a year. Fiscal reform needs more time, because an efficient tax-collection system cannot be created overnight and because there is always an unavoidable lag in collecting taxes. The experience of Poland, however, shows that it is not impossible to achieve budgetary consolidation very rapidly.

The privatization of the industrial sector (as opposed to real estate) is the biggest obstacle to a fast transition. Selling enterprises one by one is a very lengthy process—as shown by the experience of the *Treuhand* in the former German Democratic Republic—and is, in any case, not likely to yield large revenues for the government. We therefore propose that state-owned enterprises be transformed into joint-stock companies, the shares of which (or at least a majority of shares) would be given away, either to all citizens or to workers in the enterprises themselves. Privatization through "workers' shares" would have the additional advantage of bypassing the ownership dispute between the Union and the republics.

A partial (in some cases total) cancellation of corporate debt is necessary to establish a viable banking sector and to ensure that enterprises can invest without being burdened by excessive debts left over from the central-planning period.

Experience shows, however, that another, big problem is likely to arise in the transition: new laws are easily passed, but they have to be implemented and administered. This can be done only by a bureaucracy that sticks to the "market" spirit of the new laws. The quality of the existing bureaucracy and its willingness to adapt to the new rules will therefore be a crucial factor in the success of the entire reform process. The lack of a legal tradition under the rule of law, as opposed to a rule of administrative decrees in the Soviet Union, is a formidable obstacle to effective reform.

The political situation in the Soviet Union changes almost daily, but the events over the winter of 1990-91 suggest that the Union government is neither willing nor able to implement a "big bang." In contrast, the republics are gaining in strength and confidence, and their governments seem to be more committed to implement a radical reform.

This leads us to ask whether all republics have an interest in remaining in a Soviet economic and monetary union. We find that this is definitely not the case for the Baltic Republics, because they can expect to trade more intensively with the European Community than with the rest of the Soviet Union once the immediate transition phase is over. The issue is less clear for the Ukraine and the Transcaucasian republics, because they will remain more closely integrated economically with Russia. However, given the diseconomies of scale that will arise in the administrative implementation of any centralized reform program for the entire Union, even these republics would probably gain from a large degree of economic independence.

Monetary stabilization at the Union level is endangered by the external effects that will arise if a growing number of individual republics adopt their own currencies. Inasmuch as there is a large ruble overhang, a currency reform might be the best way to keep the Soviet Union together as a monetary union.

If current per capita income is, indeed, as low as $2,000, our projections of possible growth paths for the Soviet Union reveal that even the most comprehensive reforms will not permit the Soviet Union to catch up with *present* EC income levels within a generation. If fundamental reforms are delayed, there will be little growth, even if the rest of the world were to make capital generously available. Without the reform program outlined in this paper, the outcome will be dismal growth and a foreign debt of $700 billion by the turn of the millennium.

Heavy foreign indebtedness is avoidable, however, if the Soviet Union embraces drastic reforms and opens the economy to foreign trade. We have pursued this hypothesis in an analysis of two key sectors, agriculture and energy. We have shown that the low level of agricultural production is not attributable to harsh climate and geographic conditions. With decentralization, private ownership rights, and free prices, agricultural production could be stimulated significantly and agricultural revenues stabilized. The budget would benefit, because subsidies of food consumption currently exceed 10 percent of GDP, and the external accounts would benefit by the transformation of the sector from a net importer to a net exporter. The trade-account shift could amount to over $20 billion before the end of the decade.

In the energy sector, the main task is to reduce domestic waste through pricing in line with world market prices. Current energy exports generate $12 billion in hard-currency revenues. At world market prices, the value of existing energy exports would increase to $40 billion. In addition, the potential for energy saving is such that, in spite of lower production and rapid economic growth, at least twice as much energy could be exported ($80 billion or more) by the end of the decade.

To achieve this contribution of both sectors to the trade account, which could total $100 billion or more by the end of the decade, access to Western markets and transfers of Western know-how will be required. In particular, the European Community will need to open up its agricultural markets to Soviet and other Eastern European imports. In the field of energy, a long-term political framework appears necessary for the large direct investments and transfers of technology that are a precondition for a fast recovery of exports. This is the economic rationale for the EECH that is currently being discussed.

We conclude, therefore, that the Soviet Union will not benefit from substantial Western funds without direct Western leverage over reforms. At present, the internal institutional chaos and the collapse of traditional trade patterns have created a foreign-exchange crisis, but solvency does not seem at stake. Internal reform is more important than long-term capital commitments, and the West should do everything it can to hasten the reform process. The agricultural and energy sectors are certainly two major fields in which Western technology, management, and capital would help to generate large resource savings that could reduce import expenditures and produce much-needed export earnings.

REFERENCES

Aitken, Norman, "The Effect of the EEC and EFTA on European Trade: A Temporal Cross-Section Analysis," *The American Economic Review*, 63 (No. 5, December 1973), pp. 881-892.

Balassa, Bela, and Luc Bauwens, *Changing Trade Patterns in Manufactured Goods: An Econometric Investigation*, Amsterdam, North-Holland, 1988.

Begg, David et al., *Monitoring European Integration: The Impact of Eastern Europe*, Centre for Economic Policy Research Annual Report, London, Centre for Economic Policy Research, 1990.

Blanchard, Olivier, Rudiger Dornbusch, Paul Krugman, Richard Layard, and Lawrence Summers, *Reform in Eastern Europe*, Cambridge, Mass., MIT Press, 1991.

Bofinger, Peter, "A Multilateral Payments Union for Eastern Europe?" Discussion Paper No. 458, London, Centre for Economic Policy Research, August 1990.

Brainard, Lawrence, "Reform in Eastern Europe: Creating a Capital Market," in Richard O'Brien and Sarah Hewin, eds., *Finance and the International Economy 4: The AMEX Bank Review Prize Essays*, Oxford, Oxford University Press for the Amex Bank Review, 1991.

Calvo, Guillermo, and Jacob Frenkel, "From Centrally Planned to Market Economy: The Road from CPE to PCPE," *International Monetary Fund Staff Papers*, 38 (No. 2, June 1991), pp. 268-299.

Commission of the European Communities, "The Economies of 1992: An Assessment of the Potential Economic Effects of Completing the Internal Market of the European Economy," *European Economy* No. 35, Brussels, Commission of the European Communities, March 1988.

——, "Financing Requirements of the Countries of Central and Eastern Europe and the Potential Need for Complementary Financial Support," Brussels, October 1990a, processed.

——, "One Market, One Money," *European Economy* No. 44, Brussels, Commission of the European Communities, October 1990b.

——, "Stabilization, Liberalization and Devolution: Assessment of the Economic Situation and Reform Process in the Soviet Union," *European Economy* No. 45, Brussels, Commission of the European Communities, December 1990c.

——, "Annual Economic Report 1990-91," *European Economy* No. 46,

Brussels, Commission of the European Communities, December 1990d.

Cooter, Robert, "Organization as Property: Economic Analysis of Property Law and Privatization," Berkeley, University of California, March 1991, processed.

Desai, Padma, *The Soviet Economy: Problems and Perspectives*, Oxford, Blackwell, 1987.

Dornbusch, Rudiger, "Problems of European Monetary Unification," paper prepared for Conference on European Financial Integration, CEPR/IMI, Rome, January 22-23, 1990.

Economic Report of the President, Washington, D.C., Government Printing Office, 1991.

Ellman, Michael, "The Contradictions of Perestroika: The Case of Agriculture," *European Review of Agricultural Economics*, 18 (No. 1, 1991), pp. 1-18.

Fischer, Stanley, "Seigniorage and the Case for a National Money," *Journal of Political Economy*, 90 (No. 2, April 1982), pp. 295-313.

Food and Agriculture Organization of the United Nations, *FAO Yearbook. Production*, Vol. 43, Rome, Food and Agriculture Organization of the United Nations, 1989.

Gros, Daniel, "Dual Exchange Rates in the Presence of Incomplete Market Separation: Long-Run Ineffectiveness and Policy Implications," *International Monetary Fund Staff Papers*, 35 (No. 3, September 1988), pp. 437-460.

Gros, Daniel, and Alfred Steinherr, "Currency Union and Economic Reform in the GDR: A Comprehensive One-Step Approach," CEPS Working Document No. 49, Brussels, Centre for European Policy Studies, March 1990.

———, "Macroeconomic Management in the New Germany, its Implications for the EMS and EMU," in Wolfgang Heisenberg, ed., *German Unification in European Perspective*, London, Brassey's for Centre for European Policy Studies, 1991, pp. 165-188.

Gros, Daniel, and Niels Thygesen, *European Monetary Integration: From the EMS to EMU*, London, Longman, forthcoming (1992).

Helpman, Elhanan, and Paul Krugman, *Market Structure and Foreign Trade: Increasing Returns, Imperfect Competition, and the International Economy*, Cambridge, Mass., MIT Press, 1985.

Institute of International Finance, *Building Free Market Economies in Central and Eastern Europe: Challenges and Realities*, Washington, D.C., Institute of International Finance, April 1990.

———, "Union of Soviet Socialist Republics Country Report," Washington, D.C., Institute of International Finance, March 29, 1991.

International Energy Agency, *Energy Efficiency in the USSR*, Paris, Organisation for Economic Co-operation and Development, November 1990.

International Monetary Fund, *Direction of Trade Statistics Yearbook 1989*, Washington, D.C. International Monetary Fund, 1989.

International Monetary Fund, The World Bank, Organisation for Economic Co-operation and Development, and European Bank for Reconstruction and Development, *A Study of the Soviet Economy*, Paris, Organisation for Economic Co-operation and Development, 1991.

Kaser, Michael, and E. Radice, eds., *The Economic History of Eastern Europe 1919-1975*, Vols. 1-2; Kaser, ed., Vol. 3, Oxford, Clarendon Press, 1985-1986.

Kenen, Peter, "Transitional Arrangements for Trade and Payments Among the CMEA Countries," *International Monetary Fund Staff Papers*, 38 (No. 2, June 1991), pp. 235-267; reprinted in Reprints in International Finance No. 27, Princeton, N.J., Princeton University, International Finance Section, July 1991.

Korchemkin, Mikhail, "Soviet Energy—the Uncertain 1990s," *Energy Policy* (June 1990), pp. 399-405.

Kornai, Janos, *Economics of Shortage*, Amsterdam, North-Holland, 1980.

———, *The Road to a Free Economy: Shifting from a Socialist System: The Example of Hungary*, New York, Norton, 1990.

Krugman, Paul, "Increasing Returns and Economic Geography," *Journal of Political Economy*, forthcoming (1991).

Lipton, David, and Jeffrey Sachs, "Creating a Market Economy in Eastern Europe: The case of Poland," *Brookings Papers on Economic Activity*, No. 1 (1990), pp. 75-133.

Ludlow, Peter, and Helen Ross, "An Energy for the Future Europe," *Financial Times*, October 24, 1990.

Möbius, Uta, and Dieter Schumacher, "Eastern Europe and the European Community: Trade Relations and Trade Policy with regard to Industrial Products," paper prepared for the Joint Canada Germany Symposium, Toronto, November 1990.

Mundell, Robert, "A Theory of Optimum Currency Areas," *The American Economic Review*, 51 (No. 3, September 1961), pp. 657-665.

Olson, Mancur, *The Rise and Decline of Nations: Economic Growth, Stagflation, and Social Rigidities*, New Haven, Yale University Press, 1982.

PlanEcon, "How Big Are the Soviet and East European Economies?" *PlanEcon Report*, 6 (No. 52), December 28, 1990.

Sachs, Jeffrey, "Economic and Political Transformation in the Soviet Union and Eastern and Central Europe: The Role of the European Community," contribution to the CEPS Seventh Annual Conference, Brussels, November 15-16, 1990.

Sagers, Mathew, ed., *The Long-Term Energy Outlook*, Washington, D.C., PlanEcon, Winter 1990.

Shiller, Robert, Maxim Boycko, and Vladimir Korobov, "Popular Attitudes Toward Free Markets: The Soviet Union and the United States Compared," *The American Economic Review*, 81 (No. 3, June 1991), pp. 385-400.

Steinherr, Alfred et al., *Reforms in Eastern Europe and the Role of the Ecu*, Paris, Ecu Banking Association, June 1990.

Steinherr, Alfred, and Christian Huveneers, "Universal Banks: A Prototype of Successful Banks in the Integrated European Market," Research Report No. 2, Brussels, Centre for European Policy Studies, 1990.

Tirole, Jean, "Privatization in Eastern Europe: Incentives and the Economics of Transition," Massacusetts Institute of Technology, February 1991, processed.

United States Department of Agriculture, *USSR Agriculture and Trade Report*, Washington, D.C., Government Printing Office, 1990.

Willig, Robert, "Anti-Monopoly Policies and Institutions," United States Department of Justice, Washington, D.C., March 1991, processed.

PUBLICATIONS OF THE
INTERNATIONAL FINANCE SECTION

Notice to Contributors

The International Finance Section publishes papers in four series: ESSAYS IN INTERNATIONAL FINANCE, PRINCETON STUDIES IN INTERNATIONAL FINANCE, and SPECIAL PAPERS IN INTERNATIONAL ECONOMICS contain new work not published elsewhere. REPRINTS IN INTERNATIONAL FINANCE reproduce journal articles previously published by Princeton faculty members associated with the Section. The Section welcomes the submission of manuscripts for publication under the following guidelines:

ESSAYS are meant to disseminate new views about international financial matters and should be accessible to well-informed nonspecialists as well as to professional economists. Technical terms, tables, and charts should be used sparingly; mathematics should be avoided.

STUDIES are devoted to new research on international finance, with preference given to empirical work. They should be comparable in originality and technical proficiency to papers published in leading economic journals. They should be of medium length, longer than a journal article but shorter than a book.

SPECIAL PAPERS are surveys of research on particular topics and should be suitable for use in undergraduate courses. They may be concerned with international trade as well as international finance. They should also be of medium length.

Manuscripts should be submitted in triplicate, typed single sided and double spaced throughout on 8½ by 11 white bond paper. Publication can be expedited if manuscripts are computer keyboarded in WordPerfect 5.1 or a compatible program. Additional instructions and a style guide are available from the Section.

How to Obtain Publications

The Section's publications are distributed free of charge to college, university, and public libraries and to nongovernmental, nonprofit research institutions. Eligible institutions may ask to be placed on the Section's permanent mailing list.

Individuals and institutions not qualifying for free distribution may receive all publications for the calendar year for a subscription fee of $30.00. Late subscribers will receive all back issues for the year during which they subscribe. Subscribers should notify the Section promptly of any change in address, giving the old address as well as the new.

Publications may be ordered individually, with payment made in advance. ESSAYS and REPRINTS cost $6.50 each; STUDIES and SPECIAL PAPERS cost $9.00. An additional $1.25 should be sent for postage and handling within the United States, Canada, and Mexico; $1.50 should be added for surface delivery outside the region.

All payments must be made in U.S. dollars. Subscription fees and charges for single issues will be waived for organizations and individuals in countries where foreign-exchange regulations prohibit dollar payments.

Please address all correspondence, submissions, and orders to:

International Finance Section
Department of Economics, Fisher Hall
Princeton University
Princeton, New Jersey 08544-1021

List of Recent Publications

A complete list of publications may be obtained from the International Finance Section.

76

168. Paul Mosley, *Conditionality as Bargaining Process: Structural-Adjustment Lending, 1980-86.* (October 1987)
169. Paul Volcker, Ralph Bryant, Leonhard Gleske, Gottfried Haberler, Alexandre Lamfalussy, Shijuro Ogata, Jesús Silva-Herzog, Ross Starr, James Tobin, and Robert Triffin, *International Monetary Cooperation: Essays in Honor of Henry C. Wallich.* (December 1987)
170. Shafiqul Islam, *The Dollar and the Policy-Performance-Confidence Mix.* (July 1988)
171. James M. Boughton, *The Monetary Approach to Exchange Rates: What Now Remains?* (October 1988)
172. Jack M. Guttentag and Richard M. Herring, *Accounting for Losses On Sovereign Debt: Implications for New Lending.* (May 1989)
173. Benjamin J. Cohen, *Developing-Country Debt: A Middle Way.* (May 1989)
174. Jeffrey D. Sachs, *New Approaches to the Latin American Debt Crisis.* (July 1989)
175. C. David Finch, *The IMF: The Record and the Prospect.* (September 1989)
176. Graham Bird, *Loan-loss Provisions and Third-World Debt.* (November 1989)
177. Ronald Findlay, *The "Triangular Trade" and the Atlantic Economy of the Eighteenth Century: A Simple General-Equilibrium Model.* (March 1990)
178. Alberto Giovannini, *The Transition to European Monetary Union.* (November 1990)
179. Michael L. Mussa, *Exchange Rates in Theory and in Reality.* (December 1990)
180. Warren L. Coats, Jr., Reinhard W. Furstenberg, and Peter Isard, *The SDR System and the Issue of Resource Transfers.* (December 1990)
181. George S. Tavlas, *On the International Use of Currencies: The Case of the Deutsche Mark.* (March 1991)
182. Tommaso Padoa-Schioppa, ed., with Michael Emerson, Kumiharu Shigehara, and Richard Portes, *Europe after 1992: Three Essays.* (May 1991)
183. Michael Bruno, *High Inflation and the Nominal Anchors of an Open Economy.* (June 1991)
184. Jacques J. Polak, *The Changing Nature of IMF Conditionality.* (September 1991)

PRINCETON STUDIES IN INTERNATIONAL FINANCE

52. Irving B. Kravis and Robert E. Lipsey, *Toward an Explanation of National Price Levels.* (November 1983)
53. Avraham Ben-Basset, *Reserve-Currency Diversification and the Substitution Account.* (March 1984)
°54. Jeffrey Sachs, *Theoretical Issues in International Borrowing.* (July 1984)
55. Marsha R. Shelburn, *Rules for Regulating Intervention under a Managed Float.* (December 1984)
56. Paul De Grauwe, Marc Janssens and Hilde Leliaert, *Real-Exchange-Rate Variability from 1920 to 1926 and 1973 to 1982.* (September 1985)
57. Stephen S. Golub, *The Current-Account Balance and the Dollar: 1977-78 and 1983-84.* (October 1986)
58. John T. Cuddington, *Capital Flight: Estimates, Issues, and Explanations.* (December 1986)

59. Vincent P. Crawford, *International Lending, Long-Term Credit Relationships, and Dynamic Contract Theory*. (March 1987)
60. Thorvaldur Gylfason, *Credit Policy and Economic Activity in Developing Countries with IMF Stabilization Programs*. (August 1987)
61. Stephen A. Schuker, *American "Reparations" to Germany, 1919-33: Implications for the Third-World Debt Crisis*. (July 1988)
62. Steven B. Kamin, *Devaluation, External Balance, and Macroeconomic Performance: A Look at the Numbers*. (August 1988)
63. Jacob A. Frenkel and Assaf Razin, *Spending, Taxes, and Deficits: International-Intertemporal Approach*. (December 1988)
64. Jeffrey A. Frankel, *Obstacles to International Macroeconomic Policy Coordination*. (December 1988)
65. Peter Hooper and Catherine L. Mann, *The Emergence and Persistence of the U.S. External Imbalance, 1980-87*. (October 1989)
66. Helmut Reisen, *Public Debt, External Competitiveness, and Fiscal Discipline in Developing Countries*. (November 1989)
67. Victor Argy, Warwick McKibbin, and Eric Siegloff, *Exchange-Rate Regimes for a Small Economy in a Multi-Country World*. (December 1989)
68. Mark Gersovitz and Christina H. Paxson, *The Economies of Africa and the Prices of Their Exports*. (October 1990)
69. Felipe Larraín and Andrés Velasco, *Can Swaps Solve the Debt Crisis? Lessons from the Chilean Experience*. (November 1990)
70. Kaushik Basu, *The International Debt Problem, Credit Rationing and Loan Pushing: Theory and Experience*. (October 1991)
71. Daniel Gros and Alfred Steinherr, *Economic Reform in the Soviet Union: Pas de Deux between Disintegration and Macroeconomic Destabilization*. (November 1991)

SPECIAL PAPERS IN INTERNATIONAL ECONOMICS

15. Gene M. Grossman and J. David Richardson, *Strategic Trade Policy: A Survey of Issues and Early Analysis*. (April 1985)
16. Elhanan Helpman, *Monopolistic Competition in Trade Theory*. (June 1990)

REPRINTS IN INTERNATIONAL FINANCE

24. Peter B. Kenen, *Forward Rates, Interest Rates, and Expectations under Alternative Exchange Rate Regimes*; reprinted from *Economic Record* 61, 1985. (June 1986)
25. Jorge Braga de Macedo, *Trade and Financial Interdependence under Flexible Exchange Rates: The Pacific Area*; reprinted from *Pacific Growth and Financial Interdependence*, 1986. (June 1986)
26. Peter B. Kenen, *The Use of IMF Credit*; reprinted from *Pulling Together: The International Monetary Fund in a Multipolar World*, 1989. (December 1989)
27. Peter B. Kenen, Transitional Arrangements for Trade and Payments Among the CMEA Countries; reprinted from *International Monetary Fund Staff Papers* 38 (2), 1991. (July 1991)